The
CHRISTIAN PHILOSOPHY
OF HISTORY

THE UNIVERSITY OF CHICAGO PRESS · CHICAGO

THE BAKER & TAYLOR COMPANY · NEW YORK
THE CAMBRIDGE UNIVERSITY PRESS · LONDON

The
CHRISTIAN PHILOSOPHY
OF HISTORY

By

SHIRLEY JACKSON CASE

THE UNIVERSITY OF CHICAGO PRESS

CHICAGO · ILLINOIS

PREFACE

TODAY many persons are sobered by the threat of disaster to our civilization. How to avert impending calamity is a question of serious moment. The situation is especially disturbing for the religious man. His customary trust in God and his confidence in the ultimate triumph of goodness are hard to maintain in the face of adverse circumstances. For the moment evils prevail and righteousness is forced off the highway of life. It is difficult to preserve that imperturbable demeanor which Robert Louis Stevenson ascribes to quiet minds going on "in fortune or misfortune at their own private pace, like a clock during a thunderstorm." In days when the thunderclouds of war darken all skies and stretch from pole to pole, quietude of mind is a luxury that few people who take life seriously are able to enjoy.

There is one source of knowledge upon which we might draw to help us steady our perspective and define our task in times of perplexity. In the excitement of the moment we may forget the heritage of wisdom and experience bequeathed to us by the past. If we turn to history, it may brace our minds and strengthen our determination to maintain a bold front against threatening evils.

History, as understood in these pages, is the totality of remembered events that have emerged in connection

17761

with the life of mankind on earth. We have endeavored to free the study of history from the perversions that have too generally resulted when some type of metaphysical theory is forcibly imposed upon dependable historical data. When the past as actually experienced by successive generations of men is recovered and liberated from bondage to one or another speculative hypothesis, what is its significance for the making of religion today? This is the question we have tried to answer.

Our answer has issued in a call for more persistent and devoted activism on the part of mankind. History proves to be a tonic, not a sedative. God is discovered working within history, where he has willed that men should learn to be the efficient instruments of the divine energy. Upon their shoulders has been placed the responsibility for learning and pursuing God's designs for bringing his kingdom to realization on earth. This reading of the past might be regarded as a simple exposition of the Pauline injunction: "Work out your own salvation with fear and trembling, for it is God who worketh in you both to will and to work for his good pleasure."

SHIRLEY JACKSON CASE

FLORIDA SCHOOL OF RELIGION
LAKELAND, FLORIDA

CONTENTS

CONTENTS

CHAPTER I

THE CHALLENGING WORLD

LIFE in the present world is a constant challenge. The forces of good and evil seem to be locked in a perpetual struggle for supremacy over mankind. We enter life with an implicit faith in the benevolence of the universe. We assume it to be a good world that invites our trust, elicits our energy, and beckons us on to success. But presently we discover a less kindly environment in which life can be maliciously cruel. Believing, as we fain would, that we live in a good world, there is no blinking the fact that we also live in a bad world.

Everyone is involved in the conflict between good and evil. No one can stand on the side lines indifferently watching the progress of the game. All are participants, each contributing his share to ultimate victory or defeat. Our attitudes may vary. We may trust to chance or resort to cunning in our desire to avoid open conflict with the vicious forces that threaten us. Or we may adopt compromise in the hope of making the going a little more comfortable on the rough highway of life. Or, in a more heroic mood, we may boldly give battle to the enemy in a determined effort to overcome evil with good.

The world in which we live today has been a long

time in the making. Both good and evil are ancient heritages. Whether they have kept equal pace with each other in their growth or in their diminution, whether good has increased while evil has declined, or whether evils have multiplied at the expense of goodness are questions that have been and still are very differently answered. Our philosophy of life is mainly determined by our opinion as to whether the world is growing better or worse.

One favorite mode of escape from the bad world of today is the widely prevalent attempt to restore the imaginary happy conditions of days gone by. It has been a common disposition of mankind to idealize the past and deplore the present. The ancient Greeks invented the picture of a succession of world ages, beginning with the age of gold, followed by one of silver and then one of bronze, until finally the present age of iron dawned upon a distressed humanity. In the earlier periods of history there had been giants and heroes, but today only common mortals remained. Similarly, the Hebrews imagined that the beginnings of life on earth traced back to the happy abode of a Garden of Eden, wherein the first man and the first woman lived in comfort and innocence. But they fell from this high estate, dragging down with them all of their descendants to the hard life of toil and suffering. The patriarchs of antiquity had lived for hundreds of years, but now the span of life had been shortened to a brief threescore years and ten. The course of physical and social development had been one of gradual de-

[2]

terioration and increasing distress. An idealized past had been supplanted by a decadent present.

This pessimistic view of the processes of life still pervades large areas of our thinking. We feel ourselves continually overshadowed by the greater things that have been; at best we can hope to reflect but dimly the glories of the past. Our highest ambition is to approximate, as nearly as we can, the idealized excellencies of our noblest ancestors. We would repeat in our own feebler fashion the political ideals and policies of a George Washington. We would, if we could, write the English of a Shakespeare, paint the fresco of a Michelangelo, compose the music of a Beethoven, and live the consecrated life of a Jesus of Nazareth. But, conscious of our inability to perform perfectly any of these accomplishments, we strive only for a life of imitative mediocrity.

Hence, we aim to live by rules that are supposed to have been already deposited somewhere upon the pages of history. Previous custom has fixed the propriety of all thinking and action suitable for life today. Our first duty is to become intelligently aware of the precepts that have been propounded by our ancestors, and the ultimate goal of our ambition is to approach as nearly as possible to a life of conformity with these given regulations. One may seek this normative guidance from the Bible, from the Constitution of the United States, or from the enactments of last year's legislature. In any event, the procedure is inspired by the same fundamental principle. The past is thought to have been so much wiser than the present that norms for opinion and conduct have been properly fixed for all time to come by the authoritative decrees of the ancients.

In the sphere of religion the authority of antiquity has remained most strongly fortified. All religious beliefs and practices are commonly justified on the ground that ultimately they came to mankind through the processes of a revelation delivered in ancient times. The moral ideals embodied in the Ten Commandments are said to have been written on tablets of stone by the finger of God and given to Moses for the instruction of the people in all future ages. The ancient prophets, speaking in the name of the Lord, addressed to their contemporaries messages that have been credited with permanent validity. The teachings of Jesus delivered to his disciples in Palestine nineteen hundred years ago have become the norm for all later Christian life and action. Paul's letters to first-century Christian groups scattered about the old Roman world have been used as handbooks of guidance for all subsequent generations. This accumulated body of ancient writings, assembled into a single volume and canonized by the church, has acquired the sanctity of an inspired scripture—an embodiment of the truth once for all delivered to the saints. When the religious man seeks wisdom for the direction of thought and conduct in the twentieth century, he turns, by force of habit, to these records of the past for his standards and ideals.

That, he infers, was the golden age of wisdom which a degenerate present must ever strive to restore.

The organized activities of religion follow the same course. One church justifies its establishment and procedures on the hypothesis that Jesus designated Peter as the rock on which the church was to be founded; and therefore Peter's successor, in the person of the pope of Rome, is the ultimate authority in all ecclesiastical affairs. Another church holds to the primacy of the apostolic group as a whole, of whom Peter was only one of the members; and thus religious authority resides in an apostolic succession of bishops, proceeding in a direct line of descent from the official companions of Jesus. Still another church follows the Pauline pattern of administration by elders or presbyters. But whether it be Roman Catholics, Episcopalians, Presbyterians, or any other denominational group, each professes to reproduce an ancient model. It is assumed that a religious institution can have validity only when accredited by antiquity.

Religious beliefs are tested by the same standard. When systems of doctrine are formulated, they have to be fortified at every vital point by reference to biblical texts. When a new truth emerges out of some area of modern knowledge, an effort is made to show that it was contained, at least in germ, in the ancient revelation, where it lay undeveloped until brought out into the full light of day in more recent times. If the church undertakes a new task, such as the application of religion to present-day social problems, justification for

[5]

the procedure is sought in words spoken by some old Hebrew prophet or in the message of Jesus. Ancient truth is credited with a fulness, a richness, and a perfection of unsurpassable excellence, while today's religious insights and aspirations can be at best only a replica of the past.

And so we continue to live under the shadow of antiquity. The great and good things of the days of old are remembered for the inspiration and guidance of these later and less fortunate times. We cull from the pages of history the more adorable figures of the past and set them on pedestals to be admired and imitated. Their words of wisdom are cherished for the instruction of each new generation of youth. Their exemplary lives are lauded as models of conduct for worthy living today. The deeds accomplished by them are thought to constitute a solid foundation on which to rear a modern social order. The shortcomings and perversities of present-day life mark a departure from the standards of the ancients and are capable of correction in so far as we can effect an approximate restoration of the older ideals and patterns of conduct. Life today is thus generously endowed with heritages from antiquity. Although we must live in the present, it is our privilege to be, in large measure, children of the past. Out of this treasure-house of memory we seek to bring forth things both new and old for the enrichment of modern life.

Man is not only a creature of memory; he is also possessed of imagination. With the eye of creative fancy he strives to peer into every region of the unknown. Blank areas of information about the past are filled in cautiously or recklessly by the exercise of inventive skill. The scattered data of history are woven into a continuing nexus of events fabricated in accordance with some assumed laws of succession that are thought to reveal the purpose and ultimate meaning of the whole. Similarly, contemporary happenings are mutually related to one another in an effort to supply an imaginary integration of the total phenomena of present-day living that will reveal its inner significance. Even the future is brought within the domain of venturesome speculation. An attempt to forecast the probable course of coming events from the perspective of the past entices many a serious thinker. He seeks to discover the laws that will operate in the making of future history, to plot the curve that will be described by the continued operation of cause and effect, and to forecast the final goal toward which the processes of life are ultimately directed. All of which means that man is naturally inclined to be a philosopher of history.

Outlooks on the future are subject to wide variations of opinion. Few, if any of us, are so thoroughly objective in our judgment of things to come that our conclusions are not largely colored by the local circumstances of the moment or by our temporary personal emotions. Immediate desires, recent attainments or disappointments, or some cherished ambition sets the direction for thinking. Youth may paint the picture in rosy hues; middle age may make it a blend of light and shadow; while older men may view with distrust the prospects of an age that will have to be shaped without the skilful touch of their guiding hand. One who has experienced the defeat of cherished plans may see only more trouble ahead, while one who has happened to realize the goal of his desire for today may construct a quite imaginative picture of better things in the future. Whether the world is growing better or worse, whether living will be more or less comfortable tomorrow than it has been today, whether there is real progress in history or merely aimless flux—these are questions that yield no final solution when seen only with the short-range vision of single individuals and answered in terms of their accidental personal experience.

A surer hope for successful living in the future is commonly associated with the perpetuation of our numerous cultural institutions. In politics, industry, commerce, education, religion, and all phases of social activity the machinery of a continuing organization has been devised to conserve the values of the past, to augment them in the present, and to insure their endurance for days to come. These establishments, it is assumed, will counteract the transitoriness of personalities and continue the momentum of historical progress. They provide experience and training for the youth of today who are to bear tomorrow's responsibilities. They insure the longevity of skill and culture against the processes of decline and decay that all too

autumn days of civilization. Its fruits have ripened and fallen; its foliage has been smitten with the frost of approaching winter; and its vital energy is slowly but surely sinking down into the grave of eternal night. If he cherishes any hope at all, it rests upon faith in the complete collapse of the present order of existence and the miraculous establishment of a new world that will be entirely different in its structure from the one in which we live today. In religious thinking, where this doctrine has sometimes flourished, it is known as "eschatology" or "millenarianism." The multiplying evils of the present day are welcomed as a sign that the world is coming to an end. We are now living in the darkest hours of the night, immediately preceding the dawn of a new age presently to be inaugurated by the catastrophic intervention of God. Or, if this hope is rejected, there remains only the prospect of a return to primeval chaos.

The optimist offers a different interpretation of the situation. He lives in civilization's springtime. It is his faith that the things that have been are only the prelude to better things yet to be. Death, as he views it, is always followed by a new resurgence of life. Individuals and institutions may pass away, but their passing will be attended by the rise of others more competent to function effectively in the world of tomorrow. The children of each generation, when grown to maturity, will further enrich the heritages bequeathed them by their fathers. The struggle between good and evil may be long drawn out, but the champions of goodness are not pressed for time. The years that have passed thus far mark only the first step in the long course of the ages yet to come. Men move on and off the stage of history only to be followed by an innumerable host of actors yet unborn. "Time flies you say; ah no, alas, time stays, we go," and our place is taken by succeeding generations, age on age, throughout the cycles of illimitable years.

The optimist does not hope to plant his flag victoriously on the battlements of heaven in a single day or in one century. He is content if he can add but an iota to the sum of the world's accumulating experience. Advance may be so gradual that it can scarcely be seen with the naked eye; only under the magnifying glass of a long historical perspective can the forward movement be observed. Only by comparing the present status of civilization with that of a hundred years ago, or a thousand years ago, or by allowing one's gaze to range over the whole course of known time from the days of the cave man to the present can history be seen in its true light. Thus the optimist soars above the perplexing panorama of transient men and atomistic events to survey the scene in its totality. The successful journey already made by mankind from the days of primitivity to the present advanced stages of culture in a world that still has innumerable centuries of life ahead seems a sufficient guaranty for faith in the future.

What actually lies ahead of us in life must ever remain uncertain. Fears may be proved groundless, or confidence may be sadly betrayed by the ultimate outcome. At best we can but strive to possess ourselves of all available wisdom from the past, to shape the course of life today in accordance with our best judgments, and to face the coming days with whatever measure of anxiety or assurance our temperaments permit. If we are prone to place trust chiefly in the remedial permanence of institutions, it will be well for us to remember that they are always created and maintained by individuals; consequently, their efficiency can never transcend the virtues of those by whom they are made and operated. If we are inclined to think only of our personal interests, we shall need to be reminded of the fact that society is a co-operative enterprise and the welfare of the individual can never be completely isolated from that of the group. To make today's life, both individually and socially, a substantial foundation on which to build tomorrow's good is the surest ground for future living.

This ideal expressed in Christian language is the hope of the coming of the Kingdom of God. Nineteen hundred years of history leave its advent still an unrealized ambition. The conflict between good and evil continues to be waged. Men strive to live by norms drawn from an idealized past, and their hopes still remain unfulfilled. Others struggle to make of the present a better day than ever yet has been, only to discover that their ideals are a fleeing goal ever beckoning them on to harder tasks in the future. Optimism and pessimism contend for the possession of their spirits.

They are tempted to form judgments on the basis of a short-range vision and yet are unable to set limits to the endurance of time. The unknown future always looms up before them with its untried possibilities. There is no hope of escape from its uncertainties, whether one chooses to approach it with alarm or to enter its portals with confidence. These are perplexities that still challenge the skill and the wisdom of the Christian philosopher of history.

CHAPTER II

THE PROVIDENTIAL VIEW OF HISTORY

ACCORDING to the traditional Christian view of the world, God makes history. He stands at the beginning and at the end of time; and in the intervening area, where the course of temporal events is being shaped, providential guidance is continually operative. This is the major premise on which the older Christian interpretation of history is based.

The manner of God's action, however, is a subject about which there have been wide variations of opinion. Some interpreters have specified relatively definite limits for the beginning and end of time, while others have visualized an indefinitely long period approaching infinity. Also, the method of divine action in the affairs of the world has been described in many different ways. Sometimes God is assumed to be constantly present in history, overruling all events for the accomplishment of his inscrutable purposes. At other times chief stress is placed upon his occasional interference by way of unique revelations of his will injected into an order of existence that is essentially foreign to his nature—if not, indeed, dominated by hostile powers of darkness. Thus, two historical streams are to be sharply differentiated from each other—one secular and the other sacred.

Revelation, too, has been variously defined. It may be seen chiefly manifest in certain unusual occurrences, like the calling of the Hebrew people, the preaching of the great prophets, the incarnation of Christ, the establishment of the church, and similarly miraculous events supported by the scriptural records. Or it may be a more continuous process of divine manifestation welling up within the experience of the spiritual geniuses of all time, or an utterance of the still small voice within the soul of every morally and religiously sensitive individual, or even displays of the Divine Presence within the orderly processes of human reason and physical nature.

There have also been different ways of reading the designs of Providence in history. While the Supreme Deity is always thought to be the implacable foe of evil, his program for its temporary suppression and final elimination has varied with different interpreters. It has been phrased in political imagery as the establishment of a theocratic kingdom on earth that would triumph over or supplant all rival and satanically inspired regimes. Others have seen the Kingdom of God coming to realization by means of the increasing influence of the church ultimately destined to dominate the world. Or, again, on the principle that the Kingdom of God is "within you," the consummation of providential history looks toward the day when all men shall individually serve the Lord in purity of heart. Still others think that God's final purpose is the building of a regenerated human society not necessarily

[15]

identical with any branch of the church but including all mankind in a common fellowship of well-ordered living.

Throughout nineteen hundred years Christian thinking on these problems has been gradually running its course. Its real genius and further significance can be adequately understood only by surveying the main stages through which it has passed and the conditions by which it has been shaped.

A. THE HEBREW VIEW OF HISTORY

Voltaire is said to have coined the phrase "philosophy of history" in the eighteenth century; but the idea was current many centuries earlier, particularly in the thinking of the Hebrews. In their view God had intervened at the beginning of time to set the physical universe in order and to create the first human pair whose descendants were to shape the course of history. Thereafter God and men co-operated in the development of civilization. At the very outset evil also intruded itself into the picture, and the earth became the arena in which a constant conflict was to be waged between the powers of light and darkness. Man, left to himself, was doomed to defeat in this struggle; but from time to time God came to the aid of mortals. While he permitted them to suffer many afflictions in punishment for their sins, he never abandoned his concern for the preservation of the righteous. At crucial moments he had rendered special assistance. He saved Noah from destruction by the flood; he called Abraham to become the ancestor of a chosen people; he summoned Moses to deliver the Israelites from their bondage in Egypt; he established the nation under David in Palestine; he led the faithful back from their exile in Babylonia; he rescued the people from threatened destruction by the Syrian kings; and he would ultimately establish the Jewish nation triumphantly in the Holy Land when all other kingdoms would be either annihilated or converted to the Jewish faith.

The story of Hebrew civilization was a long series of frustrated hopes. But the providential reading of history always saved the people from despair. The disappointments of the past and the agonies of the present were only a prelude to the better day to be inaugurated by God in the future. The gradual transition from nomadic life to permanent settlement on the soil in Canaan, followed by the attainment of nationhood, and successive conquests of the territory by invaders from Egypt, Mesopotamia, Persia, Macedonia, Syria, and Rome kept the hope of future victory in a lively state of recrudescence. Failure to attain political stability for their civilization in a world where this ideal uniformly prevailed appeared to the Jews to be so irreconcilable a misfortune that they envisaged God's final triumph specifically in terms of theocratic nationalism. History would end, as it had begun, by a special act of the Deity in recognition of his chosen people. God would restore the kingdom to Israel.

Long-continued disappointments and the exigencies of national life stimulated fresh and varied attempts to portray the manner of the kingdom's consummation. The new regime would be presided over by God himself or by one whom he would especially anoint. This Anointed One, the Messiah, was variously depicted by different thinkers in accordance with their several tastes and the particular conditions under which they lived. Generally speaking, two main types of messianic hope were cherished. The older of these envisaged the restoration of an idealized national autonomy such as had been enjoyed under the kingship of David. God would raise up from among the descendants of David a new leader divinely equipped for his task. Other interpreters, less hopeful of success under the leadership of a Davidic prince, postulated the advent of a deliverer from heaven, an angelic messianic figure, suddenly to descend with supernatural power to destroy all enemies and establish upon a renovated earth the righteous rule of God. This figure yet to be "revealed," the "apocalyptic" Messiah, would appear at the hour appointed by God for bringing the present order of the world to a close. Then judgment would be executed upon all sinners, and Jewish national autonomy would be finally reinstated. Both the Davidic and the apocalyptic types of messianic hope survived side by side among the Jews, the one or the other finding favor as it seemed better to meet local circumstances or personal convictions.

The temporal scene, stretching from creation to the advent of the kingdom, was a confused picture of light and shadow, success and failure, hopes and disappointments. Each passing century left behind it a more or less keen awareness of ideals still unattained. As earlier ages receded into a more remote antiquity, the attainments of the past were lauded and the agonies of the present were bemoaned. This disposition to glorify the past and deprecate the present resulted in a pessimistic interpretation of contemporary history. The world was thought to be undergoing a gradual process of deterioration. The multiplication of evils moved on inevitably toward the final day of judgment, when God would suddenly intervene to destroy the forces of wickedness and inaugurate a new and eternal regime of righteousness. Then time would end and eternity would dawn.

In the meantime the present earthly life was a period of preparation for the glorious future. Adorable heritages from the past were elevated to the status of divine revelation, designed to guide the action and thinking of those who were to live in later times. Written records from antiquity became an authoritative sacred scripture composed for the instruction of future generations. These records invited study and interpretation as sources of wisdom for the direction of life in the contemporary scene. Ancient institutions were perpetuated in the belief that their continued operations accorded with God's will and would ultimately insure new manifestations of his favor. Temple ritual and sacred festivals were divine establishments whose faithful observance marked the loyalty of the people to their revered past and strengthened their confidence in final deliverance from present trouble. Pious souls rejoiced that the Lord had revealed to them his law, on which they meditated by day and by night.

God's control of current history was thus somewhat limited, or at least held in suspense, by the contemporary perversities of men and the devices of Satan. The present was a kind of interim in the divine economy. Revelation had been more abundant in the past and would reach its climactic expression in the future. The men of today lived in the afterglow of the light that had dawned upon their ancestors, and they disciplined themselves as best they could in preparation for the coming of a new age. Yet they were never completely abandoned by God even amid their severest afflictions. He was still master of all events, whether good or evil. If, temporarily, he permitted the power of evil to exercise an apparently free hand, this did not mean that he had lost control of history, but only that his all-wise designs were momentarily incomprehensible to men. Perhaps demonic forces were allowed unusual liberty of action in order that they might bring down upon themselves a severer judgment, while the fiery trials of the faithful served to purify them for a more glorious reward.

The immediacy of divine guidance was never completely absent even in the darkest hour of history. Chief reliance might be placed in ancient revelation; but the contemporary teachers and interpreters of tradition, though lesser instruments of God, echoed the divine voice. Thus the accumulating oral instruction that emanated from the schools of the rabbis became an authoritative guide for today's conduct throughout all the areas of life. Personal communion with God was also experienced in public worship and private devotions, while men of more conspicuous piety were privileged, on occasion, to enjoy in a special sense the immediate direction of the Holy Spirit. As the fatal day of judgment drew near, fresh displays of spiritual energy would be revealed. God would send a chosen messenger to call the people to repentance and would pour out his spirit in abundant measure upon the surviving remnant of Israel (Mal. 3:1–16; Joel 2:28–32). Thus, for Jewish thinking, history was providentially directed throughout its entire course of development.

B. THE EARLY CHRISTIAN VIEW OF HISTORY

The earliest Christians viewed history exactly as did their Jewish compatriots. God had initiated the historical process by a uniquely creative act; he had supervised its unfolding throughout the years; and he would presently bring it to a close by instituting judgment and establishing a new age. Fully accepting these main features in the Jewish scheme of thinking, Christians devoted their attention to developing selected phases of this imagery in line with their distinctive interests.

With respect to the end of history, early Christian views were explicit and expectant. Hope centered upon the figure of the apocalyptic Messiah, whom Christians identified with the crucified and risen Jesus ex-

[21]

alted to a position of authority at God's right hand in heaven. According to the representation of Paul, whose letters written during the sixth decade of the first century are the earliest literary testimony to this revision of Jewish faith, the resurrection of Jesus and his elevation to messianic power in heaven was a new event of cosmic significance in world history. Before his descent to earth Jesus had pre-existed with God, but he had voluntarily relinquished that status of dignity in order to live a lowly life of servitude among men. Now God had rewarded him for this humility by inducting him into the messianic office in heaven, where he awaited the moment for his return to earth to execute judgment. Then all creation "in heaven and on earth and under the earth" would confess his lordship (Phil. 2:5-11).

Christians confidently looked for the dawn of the new day. This attitude was so characteristic of them that such phrases as "waiting for the revelation of our Lord Jesus Christ," "looking for God's Son from heaven," "anticipating the coming of the Lord Jesus Christ," and similar locutions served to indicate the distinctive character of the new religious movement. Already by anticipation Christians were members of the heavenly commonwealth that was presently to be realized upon earth with Christ's return. His coming was imminent; "the Lord is at hand." Therefore, it was unwise to become deeply involved in affairs of the present world. One should avoid the distracting duties of family life, since the marriage relationship belonged only to the fashion of this world, so soon to pass away. Social reforms that aimed at ameliorating the condition of the slave or at providing employments suitable to the preservation of Christian ethical standards were not to be attempted. There was no time left for the making of significant history within the limits of the present evil age.[1]

The Pauline appraisal of the "present world" was highly pessimistic. Its wisdom was utter foolishness, and its rulers were minions of Satan. God had permitted all creation to become enslaved in the "bondage of corruption," where it groaned in agony, waiting for deliverance to be effected by the return of Christ. Vainly had the demonic powers sought to preserve their dominion by accomplishing the crucifixion of Jesus. In their ignorance of God's designs they had committed the very act that precipitated their imminent downfall. For the death of Jesus made possible God's exaltation of him to messianic dignity in heaven, and thus the stage was set for the final drama of judgment and redemption. During the brief period still to elapse before the curtain would rise, the machinations of Satan would increase. Christians underwent accumulating distresses buoyed up by the conviction that no multiplication of evils was to be compared with the glorious triumph which they would present-

[1] For these familiar Pauline ideas see I Thess. 1:10; 2:19; 3:13; 4:23; II Thess. 2:2; I Cor. 1:7 f.; 7:29–31; II Cor. 1:14; 5:23; Rom. 13:11 f.; Phil. 1:6, 10; 2:16; 3:20 f.; 4:5. Other New Testament writings contain the same ideas—e.g., Mark 1:15; 9:1; 13:29 f.; Matt. 3:2; 4:17; 10:7; Luke 21:31 f.; Heb. 10:37; I Pet. 4:7; Jas. 5:8; Rev. 1:3; 3:11; 22:7, 10.

ly experience. Even death might overtake some believers; but, when Christ came, the deceased would be raised and join the living, "caught up in the clouds to meet the Lord in the air."

The delay of history in moving toward its catastrophic climax was thought to have been designed to give the Christian missionaries time to proclaim the gospel among the Gentiles. Preaching to the Jews had not at first won large numbers of converts, but Gentiles had responded more readily to the Christian summons. Thus the number of the faithful prepared to greet the Lord on his return had been desirably increased. But this, for Paul, was only an incidental success. His philosophy of past history remained inseparably bound up with the Jewish doctrine of God's peculiar concern for the descendants of Abraham. Israel's temporary rejection of Christ momentarily provided an opportunity for such Gentiles as were willing to hear the gospel to avail themselves of its privileges. So Paul made haste to complete his missionary tours through the chief centers of the Mediterranean world. The time was short, and speedy operations were necessary if the task was to be accomplished in due season. The "hardening" of Israel was only partial and temporary; God had designed that "all Israel shall be saved." Suddenly they would all turn to the gospel, since they were beloved of God "for the fathers' sake." Thus providential history would close with the restoration of the kingdom to the Jews (Rom., chaps. 9–11).

Paul and his co-workers passed off the stage, and history moved on in its leisurely fashion from generation to generation without reaching a catastrophic close. The church grew on gentile soil and diminished in Palestine. The Jews of Palestine revolted against Roman authority, only to suffer a disastrous defeat attended by the destruction of their temple in A.D. 70. Scarcely half a century had passed before a second revolt, more severely suppressed by the Romans, wiped out the last vestiges of Jewish nationalism. No Jew was any longer allowed to set foot in Jerusalem, and even the Christian church in Palestine became a distinctly gentile institution. This course of events necessitated certain significant revisions in the older Christian interpretation of history.

The new reading of future history largely eliminated the Jews from participation in the coming Kingdom of God. Their persistent refusal to believe in Christ, the popular prejudice against them that had been augmented by their resistance to the Roman government in Palestine, and the increasing predominance of gentile converts in the membership of the Christian churches—all combined to produce the conviction that God had willed to abandon the Jews. By their unbelief they had forfeited their right to a preferred position in the new age. God had forsaken them, and gentile converts were to inherit their privileges. It was in punishment for the rejection of Jesus that God had permitted the sacred sanctuary of the Jewish nation to be destroyed. The Christian missionaries were winning converts from the east and the west who would sit down with Abraham and Isaac and Jacob in the Kingdom of Heaven, while the lineal descendants of the patriarchs would be cast forth into outer darkness.

Belief in the providential direction of past history was preserved and heightened by the new Christian interpretation. Early in the second century gentile converts with Gnostic leanings had been inclined to discount the value of the Hebrew scriptures as a dependable source of religious truth; but this skeptical disposition was resisted by the majority in the church, and before the close of the century it had been rejected outright by the rank and file of Christendom. In the meantime the Jewish Bible had been transformed into a gentile Christian book. Its pages were successfully searched for passages that were now discovered to have been explicitly prophetic of more recent events. The career of Jesus and the accumulating history of the church were found to be fully accredited in the ancient records. From the day of creation God's designs had been directed toward the founding of Christianity as the final revelation of his will within the world of time.

As the Christian movement gained stability and gathered momentum, it not only discovered new meanings in God's ordering of ancient history, but it also formulated a new theory of contemporary revelation. The dawn of the Christian era signalized a fresh impact of God upon history. Paul had claimed for every believer the privilege of guidance by the indwelling

Spirit. He made decisions under the tutelage of visions and revelations; he had "the mind of Christ." Thus inspired, he could work miracles, heal the sick, speak with tongues, prophesy, and give infallible direction to the churches. But this unrestrained spontaneity on the part of individuals possessed by the Spirit was liable to result in confusion and dissension within the Christian assemblies. Restraints were necessary in the interests of regularity. Gradually the church introduced controls designed to suppress the ecstatic urge among its members and relegated these phenomena to the earlier days of its history. Thus the spontaneities of the older Christians became respectable witnesses to the fresh outbursts of revelation that had marked the inauguration of the new Christian era.

The fresh increment of divine energy that had been injected into the human scene had displayed itself most notably in the person of Jesus. As the story of his life was rehearsed by the several gospel writers for Greek readers during the last three decades of the first century, particular attention was called to events attesting his unique accreditation by God. At baptism he had been especially endowed by the Holy Spirit; during his public career he wrought great miracles; he had also been supernaturally begotten; and he had finally triumphed over death by his miraculous resurrection. His teaching carried a new authority transcending that of Moses; it was a communication of truth that had been brought down directly from God in heaven. After his death the first apostles had been similarly equipped by an unusual outpouring of the Holy Spirit divinely inspiring them to lay the foundations of the new ecclesiastical establishment. Now God had entered afresh into the making of current history.

In the course of a few decades the record of this new revelation crystallized into a body of distinctively Christian documents that took their place beside the Hebrew scriptures as a source of divine guidance for the developing church. It was a new foundation that perpetuated in more perfect form the sacred institutions of the abandoned Jews and was a more adequate medium for conveying to mankind the will of God in the shaping of history. Its properly constituted officers, its valid sacraments, its growing educational facilities, and the observance of its elaborate ritual implemented, as never before, the decrees of God for a new age. All previous revelation was summed up and significantly supplemented in the operations of the church. It provided the final program to prepare mankind for the advent of the Kingdom of Heaven.

The church, increasing its influence from year to year, making provision for the care of man's soul from the cradle to the grave, and insuring a successful entrance to the abodes of the blest in the future life, gradually came to be regarded as an enduring institution. Now one could easily dispense with the older type of apocalyptic expectation, although it was too firmly imbedded in Christian tradition to be ignored by the theologians. They preserved the idea but projected its realization into the more distant future.

They reminded the skeptical that delay was no denial of validity, for "one day is with the Lord as a thousand years and a thousand years as one day." Especially in periods of persecution, this hope flamed up afresh to comfort the martyrs and inspire in the faithful confidence in the ultimate triumph of their cause. But, when persecutions ceased and Christianity became the favored religion of the Roman state, expectations of the end of the world grew dim. Believers were content that God should order current history through the medium of the church. Its gradual expansion, both territorially and socially, meant the coming of the Kingdom of God on earth. Until the early fourth century certain Christian writers continued to reaffirm their belief in the catastrophic end of the world, but in later times this hope was only sporadically revived to offset a sense of failure on the part of the church or to fortify the faithful in seasons of unusual calamity.

C. GOD IN WORLD HISTORY

When the church had become quite at home on earth, where it increasingly participated in shaping the current social order, it began to revise its thinking regarding the providential guidance of world history. Gradually it absorbed from its gentile environment cultural acquisitions that were superimposed upon, or blended with, its Hebrew and Jewish heritages. It discovered appropriable values from the wisdom of the Greek philosophers. Its members acquired material possessions and social prestige. This ecclesiastical conquest of the earth gave the Christian God a new and more inclusive role in the direction of world affairs.

The Roman authorities had justified their persecution of Christians on the charge that the new religionists were a menace to the well-being of the state. They were thought to be chiefly interested in otherworldly concerns that made them useless—if not, indeed, a positive detriment—to contemporary civilization. Moreover, their refusal to revere the ancient gods, under whose protection the Roman Empire had established its dominion over the habitable earth, was said to have aroused the displeasure of these divine guardians. Consequently, the gods had of late been relaxing their care for the Romans. The result had been famines, floods, civil wars, and the successful incursions of barbarian invaders within the outlying boundaries of the Empire.

These accusations led some Christians to rethink their views of contemporary history. They abandoned their former social aloofness and their expectation of an early end of the world. Instead, they affirmed that the spread of Christianity meant the infusion of society by the one divine preservative element that could insure prosperity. They stressed the fact that Christians were rapidly permeating all sections of society, introducing the ideals of the Christian life into the various callings by which men ordinarily earned a livelihood. Thus Christians were, in reality, the soul that held the world together. And some interpreters were bold enough to allege that the ultimate safety of the Empire could be insured only through the official adoption of Christianity by the government. Then the supreme God of the Christians, who now stood ready to take the entire gentile world under his protection, would become the infallible guardian of the state.

Gradually the sponsorship of the Christian God was extended to other phases of contemporary civilization. As the church developed a ritual to satisfy the longing for rites to which gentile converts had previously been accustomed, it noted a striking parallelism between some of its ceremonies and similar practices of the pagan cults. These features of gentile religion were no longer condemned but were pronounced essentially good, and the Christian God was given credit in a roundabout fashion for their origin. It was said that the revelation to Moses had embraced all truth, later to find its most perfect expression in the practices and doctrines of the church. Elements of this truth had been seized upon by evil demons who taught the Gentiles to institute baptismal rites, religious meals, and other sacred ceremonies that were genuinely divine establishments, although they had been sadly distorted in the pagan observances. It was in Christianity only that the primitive revelation came to its perfect fulfilment, but the demons had fiendishly schemed to anticipate Christianity and prevent its success by earlier acquainting Gentiles with certain fragments of revelation which they had grossly perverted. Superficially observed, it might seem that the Christian rites were but late imitations of the more ancient heathen customs, when in reality the heathen rites were pilfered perversions of Christian originals prefigured in God's revelation to Moses. So argued Justin and Tertullian in the latter part of the second century.

The wisdom of Greek poets and philosophers, as it came to be more generally appreciated by Christian intellectuals, was also drawn within the pale of God's instructions to the whole human race. The divine Logos had been the real source of enlightenment from which Heraclitus, Socrates, and many Stoics had derived their inspiration. Poets and philosophers, in so far as they had approached the truth, had enjoyed an "affinity with the afflatus from God." Even Seneca had been "frequently Christian." The partial inspiration of the wiser souls among the Greeks was ardently affirmed, although it was stoutly declared that their insights had been plagiarized from the more ancient wisdom of the Hebrews. Even the revered Plato had been a debtor to Moses. But rarely had any school of Greek philosophy been so utterly erroneous as not to reflect some measure of genuinely divine truth. One could say without hesitation that philosophy had been a schoolmaster to discipline the Greeks for the reception of Christ. It was certainly in full accord with inspired wisdom that the philosophers had declared God to be the creator of all things. Augustine expressed more than two centuries of this accumulating Christian opinion when he wrote that "the very thing which is now called the Christian religion existed among the ancients even from the creation of mankind, yet not until Christ himself came in the flesh did the true religion, which already existed, begin to be called Christian."[2]

Thus the God of Christian faith became more and more truly the God of temporal culture. Both the beginning and the end of time receded farther into the background of thinking, while divine plans with reference to the shaping of history on the terrestrial plane received increased attention. Under the influence of Platonic idealism Christian philosophers stressed the incorporeal nature of the true God and shied away from the older Hebrew imagery of his realistically physical participation in mundane affairs. As pictured now, divine guidance was mediated by spiritual agents, particularly by the Logos; nor was God embarrassed by lack of time for the accomplishment of his purposes. Indeed, the process of generation might be an eternal one, so far as the spiritual universe was concerned. So Origen had surmised. But the physical universe had been created at a specific moment as a stage upon which human beings might be provided an opportunity for training in the choice between good and evil. And it would endure until this teleological purpose had been accomplished. One also assumed that there would be an end of time, but when and how this would take place had not been surely revealed. Origen held that a physical restitution, such as Jewish imagery had depicted, was quite untenable; the con-

[2] *Retract.* i. 12. 3. Justin, Tertullian, Tatian, Athenagoras, Clement of Alexandria, Origen, and Lactantius had expressed similar opinions.

summation would be spiritually attained by those who "make a gradual advance."

When persecutions had finally ceased early in the fourth century and Christianity became the favored religion of the state under Constantine, Christians took a new interest in history. They concerned themselves with its significance in the past and its making in the present. Since emperors were ardent supporters of the church, Christian bishops ventured with increasing boldness to dictate the policies of magistrates and princes. Three centuries of precarious existence in the present evil world had issued in a clear triumph for the church, and it was now discovered that God had made more extensive plans for the ordering of temporal history than had formerly been imagined. Recent Christian events now became an integral part of the total historical stream that had issued forth from God on the day of creation, that had received a new impetus with the founding of the church by Christ, that had finally triumphed over paganism by the favor of Constantine, and that was destined to flow on victoriously in accord with the divine purposes for years yet to come.

Eusebius, bishop of the church at Caesarea in Palestine from about 315 to 340, was the most noted spokesman of this new historical outlook. As he viewed the course of history, it ran back from his own day to the most remote antiquity and included in its scope all races and nations. Therefore, he sought to reconstruct a chronological framework in which to fit the story of the various gentile peoples whose careers lay outside the range of the Hebrew and Christian past. This interest led him to study the Chaldeans, Assyrians, Egyptians, Greeks, and Romans as their history was recorded in works that had been composed by Greek authors. He thus acquired materials for the construction of a chronological table synchronizing the principal events in universal history and yielding concrete evidence to support the superior antiquity of Moses. The chronological priority of Moses over all poets, philosophers, and founders of heathen cults and the apostasy of the Jews in rejecting Christ made Christianity the oldest religion in the world. It had inherited all the temporal prestige of the Hebrew religion.

The argument from chronology had been advanced a century before the time of Eusebius by Julius Africanus, who constructed a universal chronology from creation to the year 221. The author aimed to show that the origins of Hebrew religion antedated gentile civilization and, further, to forecast the probable end of the world that would bring an end to the persecution of the Christians. It was assumed that the world was to endure six thousand years from the date of creation and that Christ had been born in the year 5500. Since about two hundred years had elapsed in the meantime, it seemed to Julius Africanus that another three hundred years would bring history to a victorious close.

Eusebius sponsored a longer perspective. As he viewed the situation, God was now working his will in history through the aging church. It perpetuated a noble antiquity, and its career had been marked by a series of antecedents and consequents that had at last rendered it triumphant in the world under Constantine. History proved it to be a divine establishment. The fate that had overtaken the Jews in punishment for their rejection of Jesus gave the church the right of way among all peoples. The work of its teachers and writers constituted a dependable historical deposit, while its purity had been preserved by the condemnation of heretics. Its increasing power, even under the severe trials of successive persecutions, demonstrated its divine origin; and its authenticity was insured by a succession of bishops traceable at all of the chief Christian centers. The story of the church was the "narrative of the government of God" over a people performing brave deeds for truth rather than for nations that had defiled themselves with blood and slaughter. Christians were the athletes of religion who had won their trophies from demons, becoming victorious over invisible enemies, and now wore the crown of triumph upon their heads. They constituted a new nation, the most numerous and pious of all, "indestructible and unconquerable because it always received assistance from God."

Christianity, however, was neither new nor strange. It had been given by God to Abraham and Moses and the Old Testament prophets. In fact, universal history from the beginning had been one continuous preparation for the gospel. Moses and the Hebrew prophets had antedated the Greek philosophers "by fifteen hundred years," and the commendable doctrinal theories of these philosophers simply repeated in less original form the wisdom of the Hebrew oracles. On the other hand, the oracles of the heathen had been the work of jugglers and cheats. Under demonic guidance they had deluded mankind to believe in fate, while it was the mission of Jesus to "ransom the whole human race from this delusion." Over and above all heathen aberrations, the affairs of the universe in their totality were being administered by Providence. Christian history was world history; heathen nations and cultures, in so far as they distorted true wisdom, were only an unhappy demonic interlude in the whole.[3]

The guiding hand of God in history became constantly more evident as the imperial state church, particularly in the East, increased its hold upon the affairs of the world. Following the example of Eusebius, a succession of Christian historians continued to record the new triumphs of the church. Emperors and bishops labored in the common cause to establish more surely the Kingdom of God. In his *Life of Constantine* (iv. 24) Eusebius tells us that Constantine had called himself a bishop ordained by God to oversee the affairs of the world, while local ecclesiastics exercised their jurisdiction within the church. Eastern emperors

---

[3] Typical passages are Eusebius, *Praeparatio* vi. 11. 295; viii. 14. 386–400; x. 9. 487*a;* xi. *Praef.* 508*b.*

perpetuated this notion of the virtual supremacy of the state over the church. Both the civil and the religious order of society operated under the sanction of Heaven without any clear line of distinction between their respective spheres. By its councils the church spoke for God in all matters of belief and practice, and civil rulers enforced these decisions upon their subjects. Church and state united in imposing divine punishments upon heretics, schismatics, Jews, heathens, and unbelievers. The ecclesiastical and civil authorities operated as one instrument for implementing the will of Providence in the making of history.

In spite of the fact that the historical stream flowed none too smoothly, the confidence of the church was not shaken. The apostasy of the emperor Julian temporarily threatened the success of Christianity, but God had intervened to effect Julian's death at the hand of the Persians in the year 363. When in the next century the Eastern emperor Theodosius II was again at war with Persia, Christ came to the help of the Romans and "executed vengeance upon the Persians because they had shed the blood of so many of his pious worshipers." Again, when Theodosius II sent an expedition to Italy to suppress a certain usurper named John, it fared rather badly with the undertaking until God heeded "the prayer of the pious emperor" and sent an angel in the form of a shepherd to guide the imperial forces through impassable marshes to the conquest of Ravenna, where John had taken his stand. And the barbarians who had assisted him were later fittingly punished. Their chief was struck dead by a thunderbolt; numbers of his followers were smitten with a plague; and many of the survivors were consumed by fire coming down from heaven. In the conflict with heretics the outcome had been so controlled by God that the Catholic church maintained its ascendancy and "led all the churches and the people to the reception of its own truth." Thus, in the East, contemporary church historians, like Socrates and Sozomen, saw the hand of God in the process of current events.

In the West, faith in the providential guidance of imperial Christian history was more difficult to maintain. Barbarian invaders freely overran the territory in the early years of the fifth century, and even the eternal city of Rome was sacked by Alaric in the year 410. This was a terrific blow to Christian confidence in God's control of history. Less than a century had elapsed since Constantine had placed the welfare of his state under the protection of the Christian God, in preference to the old Roman deities; and now the enemies of Christianity could point to the harvest of disasters that had resulted from this disregard for the sanctity of Roman tradition. Under the new divinity evils had rapidly multiplied, and civilization was on the verge of collapse.

In order to give faith a longer perspective and a steadier outlook upon unhappy contemporary events, the Christian West now turned to the study of history. About the year 380 Jerome had prepared in Latin his

Chronicle, modeled after that of Eusebius, tracing the dates of the main events in world history from the birth of Abraham in 2016 B.C. down to the death of the emperor Valens in A.D. 378. A decade later he wrote a treatise on illustrious men in the history of Christianity, to refute the popular charge that the new religion had neither philosophers, orators, nor teachers of distinction. Thus history was used to demonstrate the great antiquity and cultural respectability of Christianity even before the menace of the barbarian invasions had become acute.

With the turn of the century, when pressure from the barbarians had grown more distressing, Rufinus at Aquileia in northern Italy made a Latin translation of the *Church History* of Eusebius, to which he added a section bringing the story down to the year 395. This he did in order that the minds of men "might to some extent become oblivious to their immediate sufferings by an eager desire for the knowledge of past events." It was believed that, as men realized better the directive presence of God in earlier history, they would be able still to maintain their faith in Providence even amid present calamities.

At about the same time, Sulpicius Severus of Aquitaine in Gaul composed a concise handbook of events from the creation of the world to A.D. 400. This was designed "to instruct the ignorant and convince the learned [pagans]." It stressed the high lights of Christian history in more recent times. Persecutions had ended with the triumph of the church under Constantine. The Catholic faith had successfully withstood the Arian conflict. The recent "modernism" of Priscillian intellectualism was refuted by observing that this man "had ruined his excellent intellect by wicked studies," when he should have been devoting himself to the cultivation of monkish piety. The orthodox church was seen to be a providential establishment that insured the future. Reflection upon its historical success was the surest safeguard against present distress and calamity.

D. THE AUGUSTINIAN INTERPRETATION OF HISTORY

It remained for Augustine of North Africa to produce the classic work of Western Christendom on the philosophy of history. He was keenly conscious of the heathen charge that Christianity had disastrously weakened the strength of the state. Against this accusation he vehemently protested; yet he readily admitted that the political prosperity of Rome had decayed. In fact, the process of decline had begun long before Christ had been born. Previous political success, dating back to the early days of the Republic, had been a result of civic virtue and moral rectitude. This the true God had rewarded, even though he was as yet unknown to the Romans. But lust for power, which is a demonic inspiration, had debauched Roman life and manners, and thus an enemy more powerful than any invader "had taken violent possession not of the walls of the city but of the mind of the state." Virtue was lost when it should have been maintained and supple-

[41]

mented by the practice of piety toward the true God. Failing in each of these respects, the Roman state was due to perish; its place was to be taken by the growing Christian commonwealth. The course of progress was from Rome to Christendom:

For in the most opulent and illustrious Empire of Rome God has shown how great is the influence of even civil virtues without true religion, in order that it might be understood that when this is added to such virtues men are made citizens of another commonwealth of which the king is truth, the law is love, and the duration is eternity.

So wrote Augustine in the year 412 (*Epistle* cxxxviii. 16 f.).

The fundamental principle of the Augustinian philosophy of history was elaborately worked out in his *City of God*, on which he labored between the years 412 and 426. Citizens of the "Divine City" were those who lived in conformity with the divine will, while those of the "Earthly City" were devoted to purely worldly concerns and usually sank down into corruption. Thus the human race was composed of two classes—"those who live according to God and those who live according to men." The distinguishing mark of citizenship in one or the other city was morally and intellectually determined, while in their physical existence on the terrestrial plane all were intermingled. Gradually the divine city was destined to increase as the earthly city declined. The power of Rome had furnished useful support for Christianity in the past, but this religion contained within itself guaranties of its destiny and perpetuity. Hence the fall of Rome could not affect the prosperity of the church. It was capable of surviving by its own inherent genius and of creating any needed new forms of political protection. God's will in history was inseparably bound up with the increasing triumph of the impregnable City of God. Pagan belief in the eternity of the Roman Empire had been metamorphosed into a Christian confidence in the eternity of Christendom.

Augustine believed that God would insure the social security of mankind through the agency of the church. It was the gradually expanding community of good angels and righteous men destined in time to supplant the earthly city composed of demons and wicked men. The terrestrial city had taken the form of successive world kingdoms, of which the Roman Empire was only one example. It had been better than its predecessors in that it had finally tolerated Christianity and under Roman emperors had become, at least in outward form, a Christian state. But the best and noblest form of society was to be realized not by making the Empire more Christian but by making the church more truly imperial as mankind increasingly submitted itself to the will of God. He overruled all history for the education of the human race by a process of social evolution directed toward the establishment of his kingdom on earth and the attainment of a blessed immortality in the hereafter. The church, visible and invisible, as a concrete phenomenon and a mystic symbol, was identical with the City of God and was slowly dispossessing the earthly city of its subjects and its domains. Civil government was necessary for peaceful social order, and obedience to authority was a fundamental Christian duty. But a good political administration was always of God's making, in accordance with his design to aid the prosperity and expansion of Christianity. Its success was assured without the aid of princes, but they were not excluded from its blessings "if they make their power the handmaid of God's majesty; if they fear, love and worship God." The church was no longer within the Empire, but the Empire was within the church.

Since God was completely the master of history, both evil and good were subservient to his purposes. Contemporary disasters were incident to the history of the earthly city and a consequence of the growing corruption of Roman morals. While on the terrestrial plane, members of the heavenly commonwealth also suffered from these evils. Disaster was good discipline for Christians. It served to punish them for their sins and to test their worthiness of divine grace. It was God's inscrutable way of preparing them for heavenly rewards. Yet present agonies, however much they might be exaggerated by their immediacy in experience, were in reality much less severe than they had been in more ancient times. Viewed in the long perspective of the past, the world was seen to be growing better rather than worse. To prove this thesis Augustine reviewed Roman history from the fall of Troy to the birth of Christ; and his assistant, Orosius, demonstrated the same proposition by reference to universal history from the creation of Adam to the author's own day (about A.D. 418.).

Augustine was nearly fifteen years in writing the twenty-two books of his *City of God*, which he published gradually as the parts were completed. The work of Orosius, called *Seven Books of History against the Pagans*, was designed as a kind of supplement to the argument developed by Augustine in the first eleven books of his treatise. The completed work is full of digressions, many of which seem tedious to a modern reader; but the main line of the argument is consistently pursued. Nor is it entirely original, but it is a further development of ways of thinking that had already begun to emerge. The symbolism of the two cities was borrowed by Augustine from Tyconius, who had contrasted the "City of God" and the "City of the Devil"; but the development of the idea into a universal philosophy of history was a distinctive product of Augustine's genius. Also, the notion that the Pax Romana had been divinely ordered to prepare for the advent of Christ was an earlier conception. Prudentius, an older contemporary of Augustine, had given it definite literary expression. The glory of imperial Rome filled him with awe, a glory which was now a complete Christian possession. One could now say that "the purple prostrates itself suppliant before the altars of Christ." No one could longer doubt that Rome was consecrated to Christ, "the world brought into unity by the *pax romana*."

According to the Augustinian program, God from the very outset had been continually active in the historical process. Although his supervision of society had been somewhat limited by his permitting to man the exercise of free will, God had continued to rule the world with both mercy and justice. The ills by which he allowed men to be afflicted had a disciplinary end in view. The stubborn waywardness of man had resulted in all sorts of distress that were more conspicuous the farther one penetrated into the past. More ideal conditions had matured with the rise of the Roman Empire under Augustus, and thereby the stage had been set for the coming of Christ. That event marked a new era in world history. Thus, human impulses toward good had been reinforced and, more important still, a means of obtaining sacramental grace had been provided. The spread of Christianity among the pagans had so mitigated the divine wrath that present sufferings were not to be compared with the agonies of earlier times. The barbarians might seem to be scourges of God when one's judgment was warped by lack of historical perspective, but in reality the breakdown of the Roman Empire was only God's method of making way for a larger triumph of the church. As the ecclesiastical commonwealth enlarged, earthly governments would be absorbed or abolished. The church militant, destined to become the church triumphant, was the all-efficient instrument employed by God to implement his will in history.

According to this way of thinking, the Kingdom of

God had already been instituted on earth. The millennium, pictured in older Christian tradition as a future event, had actually been inaugurated four centuries ago, when Christ began his public ministry. Since that time he had been reigning over the saints, administering his government through the instrumentality of the church. For perhaps another six hundred years his dominion would gradually increase, but already substantial progress was evident and ultimate victory was certain. Time would end, as it had begun, under the same divine supervision that had pervaded the universe throughout the entire course of its history.

E. THE SURVIVAL OF PROVIDENTIAL HISTORY

In all of its essential features the Augustinian interpretation of universal history remained the prevalent view of Western Christendom throughout many centuries. Men believed that Divine Providence had regulated the affairs of the world from the day of creation to the present moment. Demonic agents and sinful men had deflected the course of historic development into devious bypaths from which it had been rescued by God's intervention. The call of Abraham, the revelation to Moses and the prophets, and finally the incarnation of Christ, followed by the founding of the church, had brought civilization back upon the main highway of providentially ordered history. Man's role in the making of history had been relatively insignificant, apart from the responsibility that he bore for perverting the process. But even his degeneracy had been patiently overruled by God, who knew how to make evil, as well as good, serve his ultimate purposes. In the last analysis it was pre-eminently and eternally God who made all of history. Even today this is the standard faith of both Roman Catholicism and the main branches of Protestantism.

Minor details in the program of Augustine were altered from time to time to suit changing circumstances, but the substantial structure of his thinking remained unaffected. In the next generation Salvian, living in Gaul during the period when the barbarian invaders were possessing themselves of the country, further reflected upon "God's government of the world." He, too, viewed distress as the judgment of God upon the sins of men, even of Christians; but he saw remedial values in this experience. It was through hardship that we "make our way into the kingdom." The Romans, conquered by their vicious lives, had been morally worse than the barbarians and consequently had suffered greater calamities. Since the new kingdoms were to endure while the Empire declined, they were thought capable of rendering real service to the Christian cause. Similarly, Vincent of Lerins contemplated the continued expansion of orthodox Christian doctrine, enlarged by time and refined by age, throughout "ages and centuries." The hope of the world even under barbarian dominion resided in the "universality and antiquity of the Catholic church" as God's instrument for bringing his kingdom to realization. As the barbarians became increasingly the guardians of the social order in the West, Christian thinking about history readily adjusted itself to the new situation without changing its main features. Whether the "Earthly City" was a kingdom of Vandals, Goths, Lombards, or Franks did not greatly matter, since in the last resort God's designs were automatically operative only through the church.

The belief that the historical order is providentially directed through the instrumentality of the church inspired the leaders of that organization to assume responsibility for the supervision of all of society's concerns. In the West, where the political authorities failed to measure up to the duty of serving the ecumenical interests of Christianity, this obligation was assumed by the church itself. The bishop of Rome, as the successor of Peter, to whom Christ had delegated the task of founding the Kingdom of God on earth, felt impelled to assert his authority over both church and state. Leo (440–61), Gelasius (492–96), and Gregory (590–604) struggled to keep history moving surely along the course of ecclesiastical progress amid staggering conditions of social disruption. They clung tenaciously to the conviction that the hand of Providence continued to direct the affairs of the world. Even the most heinous depredations of the Evil One were subject to the will of God. Satan had no place in the church; yet all of his machinations were overruled for divine ends. This opinion was tersely expressed by Gregory in his remark that Satan was always unrighteous, but "the iniquities he proposes to commit God allows only in so far as they serve the ends of justice." History was being shaped, even in the most troublous times, by God working through the church.

A new spirit of confidence took possession of Western Christendom with the rise of the Frankish power to dominance under Charlemagne. His favorite book was Augustine's *City of God*. He felt himself to be the divinely chosen protector of the church, a friend to the friends of the popes and an enemy to their enemies. Now the two "cities" had merged into one. Church and state were no longer rival institutions operating in separate spheres in God's government of the world. Both prince and bishop were churchmen who shared a common responsibility for maintaining a Christian civilization. Kings ruled by divine right under the patronage of the church, and it was entitled to protection by the royal power which it had thus created. Both political and religious officials served within the scope of God's constructive activities in the making of history.

The conviction that the church was God's only instrument for use in establishing his kingdom, and that supervision of political administrations was also the task of the ecclesiastical authorities, inspired the long and often bitter struggle on the part of popes in the Middle Ages to dominate emperors and kings. In the sphere of the Kingdom of God the Roman pontiff was "Christ on earth," the light of the nations and the lodestar of the people, "in order that salvation might universally obtain even to the ends of the earth." So it was affirmed by Arnald of Villanova at the close of the thirteenth century. This supreme responsibility of the church for insuring a God-ordered civilization received its classical expression in the famous Unam Sanctam of Boniface VIII in the year 1302. It declared that "both the spiritual and the temporal swords are in the power of the church, but the latter is wielded for the church and the former by the church; the one by priests, the other by kings and soldiers, but at the command or with the approval of the priest."

By subjecting all political power to the authority of the church the unity and universality of God's control of history had been preserved. Yet society failed to arrive at a state of millennial perfection. The power of kings, particularly in France and England, slowly increased to the point where these monarchs resisted papal supervision and claimed to rule by a divine right received directly from Heaven. Emperors and popes fought with one another for supremacy. Even the Crusades failed to cement the multiplying diversities of European society into a unified Christian commonwealth. The forces of disruption continued to gather momentum. The facts of experience were negating the theory of a papally controlled society in which the earthly city and the City of God were fused. This version of Augustinianism needed further revision to make it accord with the unsettled state of the times.

Those medievalists who gave attention to history were usually content to compose annals quite free from philosophical reflection. But a true successor of Augustine appeared in the person of Otto of Freising, who wrote a universal history, bringing the story down to A.D. 1146. This *Chronicon*, or *Two Cities*, followed the pattern of Augustine and Orosius, except that it abandoned their optimistic outlook on the future. Otto retained full confidence in God's government of the world, but the turbulence of the times in the twelfth century convinced him that the day of judgment was at hand. Christendom itself had become so corrupted that it offered no hope for bringing the City of God to realization on earth. That could be accomplished only by a catastrophic act of Deity. It was the City of Antichrist to which the present wretched condition of the world pointed; and, when this demonic regime had reached its brief but terrible climax, God's redemption would be suddenly revealed.

The revived strain of apocalypticism continued to flourish in different areas of medieval thinking, but the most significant supplement to the providential interpretation of history came from another source within the church. The scholastic theologians who substituted the Aristotelian philosophy for the Platonism of Augustine—or perhaps one should say "superimposed the former upon the latter"—while they did not concern themselves primarily with historical theory, led the Christian mind toward a new synthesis of the totality of history. Augustine had been chiefly concerned to justify the ways of God to man; but scholasticism, especially as expounded by Thomas Aquinas, gave man a larger measure of responsibility for shaping the course of the world. While not for a moment assuming that the providential oversight of God had been in the least relaxed, or that the church, even as papally administered, was not the divine instrument for bringing the Kingdom of God to realization on earth, Aquinas stressed the dignity of human nature and the operation of man's rational free will as forces co-operating with God in determining historical events. In other words, both God and man joined hands in the providential government of the world. It followed that progress in history waited upon the wisdom and willingness of man to pursue the way of truth supremely revealed in the teaching and conduct of the church. The end might be far off; but advance toward the goal was assured, and the ultimate outcome was certain.

With the rise of Protestantism popular confidence in the providential administration of world affairs through the agency of the Roman pontiff was explicitly denied. The Protestants reverted to the Augustinian way of thinking, in which the activity of God almost obliterated any human responsibility for shaping the course of providentially supervised events. There was a sharp revival of interest in history, but for the moment its main concern was to demonstrate the decadence of the Roman Catholic establishment. The hand of God had been uniquely manifest in the primitive age of the church, but satanic influence had been increasingly conspicuous during the last thousand years. Thus, traditional Protestantism repeated without essential alterations the providential interpretation of history expounded by Augustine.

Among Roman Catholics the authority of Thomas Aquinas was reinstated by the Council of Trent (1545–63), but his significance for the interpretation of history has not been vigorously revived until within relatively recent times. Bossuet's noted *Discourse on Universal History*, first published in 1681, was mainly a reaffirmation of Augustinianism designed to glorify the Catholic church of France. And even Giambattista Vico's "sociological" reading of human history, notwithstanding its scientific sincerity, rested upon faith in the same Platonic absolute that supported the exposition of Augustine.

It has remained for the modern Neo-Thomists to defend the providential view of history by reference to the metaphysical postulates of Aquinas. They make God the ultimate ground of the historical process, the first cause, the prime mover. He is also the all-dominating overlord who controls the end from the beginning. But rational human nature and man's freedom to choose between good and evil are also conditioning factors in the making of history. God alone determines the end, but men are responsible for shaping the course. Evil does not inhere in the nature of things but is a consequence of satanic activity leading men to make choices that depart from the true wisdom taught by the church.

Thus, God still operates through the church, even

though the latter no longer controls by force either individuals or states. Rather, it is the persuasive power of the redemptive wisdom emanating from the church, and by it alone, that the future progress of history is insured. Evil cannot ultimately prevail because God turns to good account even wicked designs and actions. The devil does badly only what good folks temporarily fail to do well. And so history ever moves forward, carrying along this fiendish vampire in the historical stream but allowing him to be active only in respect to those things not redeemed by the blood of Christ. Time belongs to God, whose inscrutable purposes are always approaching fulfilment. Good and bad are still intermingled; but, as time moves on, the moment of final separation will arrive when the triumph of God will be complete and history will be at an end.[4]

[4] See, e.g., Christopher Dawson, *Progress and Religion* (London, 1929); J. Maritain, *Freedom in the Modern World* (New York, 1936); Peter Guilday (ed.), *The Catholic Philosophy of History* (New York, 1936).

CHAPTER III

THE HUMAN VIEW OF HISTORY

TOWARD the beginning of the nineteenth century men began to be more definitely conscious of their own responsibility for the making of history. Human initiative demanded, and received, an increasing measure of recognition in the political, economic, and intellectual spheres. Even in the always conservative atmosphere of religion there was a growing tendency to tolerate divergent opinions and practices sponsored by different groups acting under the conviction that their personal tastes should be determinative for their beliefs and conduct. The individual acquired a new freedom in both word and deed—a fact that immensely augmented his accountability for the shaping of the world's affairs. Gradually emphasis shifted from the decrees of God to the activities of men in molding the course of history.

The shift of interest from the transcendental sphere of the Deity to mundane actualities resulted in a type of historical interpretation more suitably termed "human," or "secular," rather than "providential," or "sacred." Human history draws its deductions from the observable facts of the recoverable temporal sequence without primary reference to what may have been in the mind of God before the beginning of time or what may be his intentions regarding the outcome of cosmic events when measurable time has issued in eternity. It may altogether refrain from concerning itself with God's relation to history, or it may attempt to read the divine mind in the concrete signs of the times. In any event, it is less interested in justifying the ways of God to man than in tracing the process of the human struggle godward. It shuns metaphysical speculation and worships at the shrine of empiricism.

A. THE SEARCH FOR FACTS

The empirical historian's first loyalty is to his available sources of information. For knowledge of events that lie beyond the range of his personal observation, his primary dependence is upon documents. Where these are lacking, history is a blank. Hence the avid search for historical records that has been carried on with increasing vigor during the past century. Attempts have been made to seek out the literary remains of every ancient culture in all parts of the world, to decipher every unknown tongue in which any document happens to have been written, and to make these sources available for study in hundreds of modern research libraries. This gigantic task has elicited the devotion of a host of scholars in various centers of learning throughout the civilized world. The assembling, the reading, and the interpretation of documents is the first task of the historian.

The literary records of the past have been extensively supplemented by digging among the ruins of ancient sites where old civilizations once flourished. These archeological excavations have uncovered vast quantities of data for use by the historian. Local inscriptions, thus unearthed, often prove very informative. The foundations of city walls, temples, theaters, and private dwellings tell their own story. Cooking utensils, temple furniture, and objects of art reveal the ancient mode of life. The images and legends on coins are suggestive of the political and religious interests of antiquity. The trappings from tombs disclose current customs and hopes that were entertained regarding life after death. Old libraries of clay tablets open up a new world of cultural activities and mental outlooks. Papyri and potsherds recovered from heaps of rubbish yield fragments of information about the business and social life of the ordinary citizen. Thus, archeology has become one of the historian's most valuable instruments for restoring a knowledge of the way in which mankind has lived and wrought out various types of civilization in every quarter of the earth's surface.

The search for facts involves more than the mere recovery of objective data. In order to rebuild the story of the past, the historian undertakes the additional task of so interpreting his archeological findings and documentary sources as to restore a picture of the actual life of people in ancient times. He must fill in numerous blanks in the records before the skeletal remains can be clothed with a vital body of reality. If, as often happens, he has only fragments of a temple column, he must judge its total shape and size from the curvature and contour of the bits that are at his disposal. From the ruins of an altar and a few ritual utensils he ventures to reconstruct a picture of the operations and meaning of an ancient religious cult. Scattered remarks from brief inscriptions, broken pieces of pottery, or tags of papyrus have to be woven into a continuous story of prevailing ways of thought and conduct. This is a venturesome procedure that severely tests the skill, vision, and judgment of every would-be reliable historian. Since he limits himself to such knowledge as is obtainable on the strictly human level, his conclusions can be only relatively correct. He may not claim for them absolute validity.

Historians nowadays have come to realize that even the bulkier type of written documents has to be viewed with a critical eye. As long ago as the fifteenth century, representatives of the new humanistic learning in Europe began to distrust certain long-accepted records from antiquity. While it was allowed that history might still have been made by the hand of God, the story of past events was seen to have been a human product liable to errors of judgment—if, indeed, it was not sometimes a deliberate invention. In the year 1439 Laurentius Valla, an Italian humanist, demonstrated that the Donation of Constantine, until then universally accepted as an accurate record of fact, was a forged document. Later he exposed the fictitious character of the correspondence between Abgar and Christ, which had been generally believed since the time of

Eusebius, who had included it in his *Church History*, Book i, chapter 13.

The necessity of critically questioning the accuracy of documents has slowly gained recognition, until today it is a universally admitted procedure for every diligent historian. Since all written records are human creations, they partake of the limitations or perversities under which their authors labored. How they are to be studied, the questions one must ask about them, and the processes by which the ultimate truth of history may be partially or wholly recovered from the imperfect or incomplete records have been made subjects of inquiry by numerous scholars who have composed either handbooks or encyclopedic treatises to guide their colleagues in the correct pursuit of historical knowledge.[1]

If history has been written by fallible men and

[1] See, e.g., E. A. Freeman, *The Methods of Historical Study* (London, 1886); C. V. Langlois and C. Seignobos, *Introduction to the Study of History* (New York, 1898); H. B. George, *Historical Evidence* (Oxford, 1909); J. M. Vincent, *Historical Research: An Outline of Theory and Practice* (New York, 1911); F. M. Fling, *The Writing of History: An Introduction to Historical Method* (New Haven, 1920); E. Bernheim, *Lehrbuch der historischen Methode und der Geschichtsphilosophie* (Leipzig, 1889, and several later editions); W. Bauer, *Einführung in das Studium der Geschichte* (2d ed.; Tübingen, 1928); A. Feder, *Lehrbuch der geschichtlichen Methode* (3d ed.; Regensburg, 1924). For the historical and critical evaluation of the new methods, see E. Fueter, *Geschichte der neueren Historiographie* (Munich, 1911); G. P. Gooch, *History and Historians in the Nineteenth Century* (London, 1913); M. Ritter, *Die Entwicklung der Geschichtswissenschaft* (Berlin, 1919); E. Troeltsch, *Der Historismus und seine Probleme* (Tübingen, 1922); Maurice Mandelbaum, *The Problem of Historical Knowledge* (New York, 1938).

passed on to posterity in recopied or translated versions of the original composition, the first duty of the interpreter would seem to be the recovery of the ancient text and a correct understanding of its language. An increasing effort to restore original texts and to comprehend the accurate meaning of the tongue in which they were composed is a commonplace among all present-day thinkers about history. Even the canonical scriptures of Christendom, originally written in Hebrew, Aramaic, and Greek and surviving today in a multitude of varying manuscripts and translations, must be subjected to the restorative process. One who would recover accurately the course of so-called "sacred history" must at least allow that secular influences have been operative in the transmission of the records, even though it should still be maintained that the original documents were more directly inspired by God. The necessity of this work of the "lower" criticism, as it has been commonly termed, is nowadays universally recognized.

The modern interpretation of history is not, however, content with the mere effort to discover, restore, assemble, and decipher original texts. Beyond the document lies the question of the dependability of the tradition which it embodied. Whether an author used oral or written sources, or both, the information that came to him may have been subject to human limitations. Lack of adequate knowledge, zeal for a favorite cause, the allurements of a vivid imagination, the influence of local circumstances, and even a sincere or perverse desire to shape the thinking of posterity may have operated to produce the traditions which an ancient author incorporated in his writings. Moreover, the accuracy—if not, indeed, the good faith—of an author is always open to question. Even if he did not deliberately distort the facts to suit his taste, he may at least have been honestly mistaken in his reconstruction of events.

One must constantly reckon with the personal equation. The situation in which a writer lived, his opportunities for assembling correct information, the purpose his composition was designed to serve, his personal likes and dislikes, and every other weakness or limitation to which human flesh is heir must be taken account of by the student of history. Thus has arisen the "higher" criticism, as it has been called, by which one seeks to go beyond the verbally accurate text to an analysis of the sources, a determination of actual authorship, a knowledge of the time and place of composition, and a judgment on the dependability of the various items of information reported in the text.

The secular approach of this "higher" criticism has now extensively invaded the domain of Christian historical thinking, including even the treatment of biblical documents. The fact of canonicity is no longer assumed to be a guaranty of accuracy. While the writers of both Old and New Testament narratives may have believed their statements to be true, one must still rec-

the point of departure for all human living. It is the arena in which individuals fulfil their destiny, and it is the soil in which their continuing influence strikes its roots and from which it bears its fruit. While one may truthfully say that men create society, they do so only as active members of the society in the process of whose making they vitally share. A century ago Thomas Carlyle could believe that "the history of what man has accomplished in this world is at bottom the history of great men who have worked here." And we may readily agree with him that they are "profitable company." But we must remember that the life of the great man is always socially conditioned both in its genesis and in its operations. Had his interests and conduct been so entirely novel as to separate him completely from the ordinary life of his contemporaries, he would have been adjudged a freak rather than a hero and would have been straightway forgotten. The history of the common herd of humanity is the substantial reality constituting the foil against which to display the alleged virtues of the genius or the hero. History includes all of them in its totality.

Consequently, the historian's search for facts embraces the entire field of man's life within his total social environment. His habits, his ideas, his activities, and his accomplishments throughout the whole course of mankind's existence upon the earth are the constituent elements of the historical picture that one seeks to restore. It includes every type of human institution—whether political, economic, religious, aesthetic, or cultural in the most comprehensive sense of the term. It embraces every skill that has been developed and every idea that has been entertained. Technology, philosophy, science, education, industry, commerce, and every other form of activity in which men have participated come within the range of the historian's vision. He aims to write the complete story of human civilization. No available fact about the past is foreign to his interest. This perfection of knowledge is a grand ambition whose fulfilment is still far from realization. Perhaps it is a fleeing goal which many future generations of scholars may desperately but vainly struggle to attain. But anyone who is content to relax the strenuous quest for facts will forfeit his right to membership in the fraternity of accurate historians.

B. THE DISCOVERY OF CAUSES

The secular view of documents was early supplemented by a tendency to interpret in a similar way the formative influences that have been operative in the making of history. Earlier scholars had assumed that their only task was to describe, as accurately as the records would permit, the happenings of the past. To determine why things had happened as they did was no part of their problem. This was the objective ideal enunciated by the famous Leopold von Ranke, who by the middle of the nineteenth century had become the Nestor of the rising generation of scientific historians in Germany. His alleged purpose was merely to make clear what had actually occurred. The statement was well meant and important as an antidote to current historical romancing and Hegelian metaphysical speculation. It brought the subject down to earth and thoroughly domesticated it on the human level. But disciples of von Ranke have sometimes been tempted to transform his wise advice into an infallible norm for all future conduct. It then becomes not only a safeguard against fictional and philosophical perversions of history but also a negation of the propriety of looking behind specific events to discover their natural or necessary causes on the historical stage of strictly human conduct.

Nowadays it has become a common procedure to seek the key to the historical process in the realm of natural, rather than supernatural, causation. To determine just what happened is only preliminary to the task of discovering the causes that induced the event. Since history is the product of social evolution and since society is always a going concern where antecedents and consequents are in perpetual motion, one endeavors to amplify historical knowledge by examining the causal nexus in which every event has its necessary setting. The happenings of the past are viewed in their proper genetic connections as the historical panorama unfolds itself before the eye of the attentive observer. Both causes and results are held to be equally valid facts of secular history.

The quest for causes has invited much speculation and experiment. There has been a prevalent temptation to oversimplify. One cause exalted above all others is made the dominant, if not the sole, formative influence shaping the total course of history. The older types of interpretation found ideas and personalities to be the determining factors in historical evolution. In this respect the heritage from Hegel was especially conspicuous. As he read the story of the past, it was the record of the way in which the absolute idea had been striving to break through from above into the temporal scene. The struggle had been a fluctuating one by which thesis and antithesis gradually culminated in synthesis. This conflict of pros and cons issued by degrees in a realization of the world's ultimate purpose, which is to manifest in itself the actual embodiment of the divine reason. Thus the providential view of history is reinstated: "Reason in its most concrete form is God. God governs the world; the actual working of his government—the carrying out of his plan—is the history of the world."

When the idea is particularized in the form of the mental activity of outstanding persons, they become the ultimate creators of history. It is said to be shaped by the persistent motives of man and the permanent habits of his mind. Thus the science of history is essentially psychological. Not only does one recognize the creative mentality of individuals, but certain abstract psychological principles are assumed to hold true for groups or classes of men, like the primitives, the hero, the genius, the laborer, the capitalist, the clan, the race, the nation, or other specific social units. Then it is only a short step to the further postulate that some dominating principle from without, like world spirit or social mind, is the ultimate factor in the making of history. Thus the providential view, though in a denatured form, is once more enthroned above the processes of historical development. History is made after some prescribed pattern a comprehension of which furnishes the key to the whole.

Many older historians believed that political aspirations had been the elemental factor in shaping the course of the historical process. Hegel had assumed that the final manifestation of his absolute idea would find concrete expression in the organization of the ideal German state. This was the goal toward which all historical development was directed. Since organized government was necessary to safeguard every form of social desire and activity, the establishment of a stable political order was the primary purpose toward which the human struggle for existence aimed. Hence, the efforts of the historian were devoted to an understanding of the origin, the development, the conditioning factors, and the task of political institutions. The information essential for this purpose was to be found in the biographies of outstanding leaders. Generals who conducted wars, kings and emperors who formulated and administered laws, the legislative enactments of ruling bodies, and the rival conflicts between nations were the matters of first importance. One who had acquired a true insight into these phenomena was thought to know the inner secrets of history.

When history came to be viewed more explicitly in terms of the complexities of the elemental social process, political institutions were seen to be the product, rather than the primary cause, of the development. All institutions represent a secondary stage in the growth of the social structure; they are devised to conserve or nourish more fundamental interests of mankind. Man is a living organism dwelling within a physical and social environment, where he is impelled in his activities by natural appetites and mental curiosity. He has, or believes that he has, powers of choice and capacities for attainment beyond what is offered to him in his immediate situation. Hence he makes history by responding to his impulses, pursuing his desires, and practicing his choices. Therefore, one who would discover the genetic causes of history must plumb the murky depths of human motives to action at these more elemental levels of conduct.

Some interpreters have found the secret of historical causation in man's physical environment. Every life has its physical setting. To say that the individual is a "child of earth" is no mere figure of speech. If his body is dust of its dust, so too is its atmosphere his life-giving breath. His food is such as its soil and its waters yield. His clothing and his shelter are its peculiar gifts. His cultural heritage is the remembered story of man's struggle for attainment within its limitations. The tasks that challenge his spirit are set by those conditions of society which it has shaped and sustained. And the ideals he cherishes come to realization only as they are translated into concrete attitudes and deeds by himself and other actual people who continue to inhabit one or another region of the earth's surface.

Shortly after the middle of the nineteenth century Henry Thomas Buckle, in his *History of Civilization in England*, sought to show how the mental and moral development of man was influenced by external forces of nature. Stressing the intimate connection between human actions and physical laws, he affirmed that greater knowledge of the latter would light up many obscure questions about formative factors that had gone into the making of history. The work of Buckle seems to modern scholars immature and sometimes naïve, but his theme has been developed in more specialized forms by several successors.

The influence of geography and climate has sometimes been strongly emphasized. It is a self-evident fact that human living is conditioned by the productivity of the soil, by the prevalence or lack of rainfall, by degrees of cold and heat, by contiguity to the sea, by the contours of mountain-encircled territories, and the like. These forces were conspicuous in determining many ancient civilizations. The river valleys in Mesopotamia and Egypt and the location of Palestine as the physical bridge between Egypt and Mesopotamia are substantial facts underlying the history of the ancient peoples who dwelt in these regions. The effect of the

Mediterranean Sea upon the history of Roman civilization is perfectly apparent. Similar observations hold good for the activity of man in every area of the earth's surface. Whether the influence of physical environment is thought to be mandatory or only passively operative, its effect upon history is an elemental fact not to be ignored.[2]

The acquisitive instincts of mankind have suggested to other modern historians that the economic quest has been the ultimate creator of history. Subsistence has always been an important problem for humanity. From earliest times individuals and groups have contended with rivals for the possession of hunting grounds, pasture lands, or other physical possessions necessary for the maintenance of life. Nations have fought with nations for control of natural resources, commercial privileges, and mastery of the sinews of productivity. Within specific social groups there has been a perpetual conflict between classes aspiring to acquire financial well-being at the expense of competitors. Just as natural selection is a fundamental law of life in the physical realm, so the economic struggle is thought to be the basal motivation in the social

[2] See, further, Lucien Febvre, *A Geographical Introduction to History* (New York, 1925); H. B. George, *The Relations of Geography and History* (5th ed.; Oxford, 1924); E. Huntington, *Civilization and Climate* (3d ed.; New Haven, 1924); Ellen C. Semple, *Influences of Geographic Environment* (New York, 1911); Franklin Thomas, *The Environmental Basis of Society* (New York, 1925); Ray H. Whitbeck and Olive J. Thomas, *The Geographic Factor: Its Role in Life and Civilization* (New York, 1932); J. Brunhes and C. Vallaux, *La Géographie de l'histoire* (Paris, 1921).

[71]

evolution of the human race. Viewed from this angle, the development of all historical institutions is due to man's desire for worldly possessions. Whether the institutions are political, intellectual, cultural, or religious, the economic urge is believed to have exerted the preponderant influence in shaping the progress of society.[3]

By the middle of the nineteenth century the doctrine of economic determinism had taken substantial form in its exposition by Karl Marx. He believed that material conditions furnished the cause of all historical movements. Leaning heavily upon the philosophy of Hegel, he sought the essence of history in the fact of struggle, but he substituted rival classes of society for the Hegelian conflict of ideas. And from his older contemporary, Feuerbach, he adopted the slogan "Man is what he eats." Reasoning from these premises, Marx found the whole history of mankind explained in terms of the struggle between the ruling and the oppressed classes. And the ideal goal of history was the ultimate triumph of a revolutionary proletariat that would redeem the world by the suppression of all opposing classes. Labor would exploit for its own benefit the entire industrial and political system. This new society, completely dominated by economic inter-

[3] For more recent typical expositions of the subject one may consult E. R. A. Seligman, *The Economic Interpretation of History* (New York, 1902); R. H. Tawney, *Religion and the Rise of Capitalism* (New York, 1926); Max Weber, *General Economic History* (New York, 1927); A. L. Rowse, *Science and History: A New View of History* (New York, 1928); H. Sée, *The Economic Interpretation of History* (New York, 1930).

ests, would mark the climax of historical development. Mankind was destined for an economic utopia.

Regardless of the judgment one may pass upon the communistic experiment in modern Russia, where the Marxian philosophy has secured its largest following, many present-day historians retain a high regard for the formative influence of economic considerations. The various institutions of civilized society rest upon a financial foundation without which they would quickly decline and crumble. Economic prosperity is the very lifeblood of our industrial order. Labor, business, law, education, religion, the aesthetic arts, national and international politics, and every cultural enterprise in which men engage depend for their success upon an adequate source of material subsistence. And, since the quest for subsistence, maintained upon the highest possible level, is thought to be the fundamental and universal aim of individual and social life, the economic motive becomes in the end the determining factor in the total process of historical evolution. Even when it is conceded to be only one among many forces actuating human conduct, it is still thought to be the most elemental and powerful influence operative in the life of mankind.

Other interpreters would attach greater significance to the creative power of man's intellectual quest. At a higher level of existence his love of truth transcends his love of money. This quality may as yet characterize the few rather than the many, but it is said to be a latent capacity due to increase with the gradual advance of civilization and will become, in the long centuries that lie ahead, the ultimate power finally shaping the course of history. Indeed, the past is rich in illustrious examples of men who have lived for the pursuit of ideals even at the price of persecution and martyrdom. Nor has their memory and influence suffered eclipse in consequence of their unfortunate fate. The Hebrew prophets were usually despised by their contemporaries, Socrates was compelled to drink the cup of poison, and Jesus was nailed to a cross—all in consequence of their unyielding allegiance to their respective visions of truth. And history ever since has been enriched by their contributions to the moral, intellectual, and spiritual aspects of human living. The mental life of man is quite as realistic a fact as is his material being. These two phases of his existence are inseparably bound together, and neither can be understood without allowing to each its due measure of influence.

History's concern with the activities of the human mind may be a more subtle quest than that which deals only with material things, but it is none the less significant for an understanding of the motives that have determined conduct. The present has been justly called a "materialistic age"; yet, even so, the dominating purposes of life do not always aim at physical satisfactions. The love of parents for their children, human sympathy for the unfortunate, the pursuit of ideals for their own sake, the devotion of the scientist to the search for knowledge, the self-giving service of the

teacher for the good of his pupils, the sacrificial life of
many ministers of religion at home or in distant lands,
and even the spirit of brotherhood inconspicuously
displayed by hosts of forgotten men—all bear eloquent
testimony to vital urges on the human plane that make
history something more than an elemental economic
drive. It is very true that man cannot live without
bread, but frequently he will go a long way toward
denying the satisfactions of the palate in the interests
of serving his appetite for intellectual, artistic, moral,
and social ideals. Even politicians are not always in-
sincere in their devotion to ideals, and they have been
known to endure much personal inconvenience in the
service of what they believed to be a just and worthy
cause.

Religion has played a large role in the making of
history. At least in theory, the religious man pledges
his primary allegiance to moral and spiritual ideals.
Just as it is only valuable coinage that inspires coun-
terfeits, so religion has often been preyed upon by the
charlatan. But, by and large, he is the exception
rather than the rule. And, since ideals are judgments
of value made according to the measure of light possessed by their adherents, they may, on occasion,
seem to have been hardly worthy of pursuit. But that
contingency does not alter the fact of their predomi-
nant influence in determining human action in the
past. The historian who ignores the moral and spiritual quests of men, whether he adjudges them worthy
or unworthy, will fail to appreciate one of the most

significant factors that have entered into the making of history.

When the genetic forces in the historical process are sought within society itself, their complexity becomes immediately manifest. No single cause can be set above all others. Variety of form and multiplicity of interaction weave themselves into an intricate pattern whose details are often difficult, if not impossible, to distinguish. One or another influence may be dominant for the moment in a specific situation, but all of them have to be taken into account to explain the total picture.

Man lives in a world of physical limitations; yet he constantly invades another world, real or imaginary, created by his mental explorations. Territory, soil, and climate may determine his food and clothing; but even these needs cannot be satisfied without some measure of intelligent co-operation on his part. As for the economic quest, he may will to pursue it or he may will otherwise. He is free to shape his political ideals in accordance with his changing tastes. He explores the realms of moral and spiritual attainment and chooses the paths he will pursue or avoid. He is ever learning by experience. This program may be called one of trial and error, or it may be termed the pursuit of experiment and aspiration. In any event, life is perpetually on the move, and its course is being shaped by multitudinous forces—some of them old and some new, some from without and others welling up from within—that generate the processes of history.

C. THE PROBLEM OF PROGRESS

When men make history, what specific end do they have in view, and in what measure are they progressing toward the attainment of their goal? Betterment has been a universal ambition. If men have not improved their status with the passing of the centuries, their failure cannot be charged to absence of desire or lack of effort. Yet they may have erred in their judgments of value, and their energies may have lagged far behind their aspirations. The fact of their failure always looms large in contrast with the measure of their success. Perhaps progress, instead of being a law of life, is only a product of man's wishful thinking.

The question of progress is no problem for the providential interpretation of history. God, who orders all the affairs of the world according to his inscrutable will, has decreed that sacred history should gradually rise to higher stages of attainment, while profane history is destined to sink down to lower and lower levels. This was the Augustinian view that has long prevailed in traditional circles of Christian thinking. As far as the natural man is concerned, his fallen condition rendered him quite incapable of improvement. Not until God intervened to introduce a new divine order of society represented by the church could there be any hope for betterment in the state of human affairs. Sacred history alone can be progressive, while secular history becomes an inevitable regression.

When the problem is transferred to the terrestrial

plane, its solution becomes less certain. Whether history reveals a gradual development toward an improved social order or discloses a perpetual futility of endeavor is an issue that has elicited a wide range of varying opinions. It is a question of the balance to be struck between the frailties of man and his capacity for self-improvement. Two types of procedure have been employed. They may be distinguished as the philosophical and the observational. The former argues from a postulated principle of progress to its concrete manifestation in history, while the latter first examines the specific phenomena of history as a basis for deductions regarding the actual emergence of progress. Both procedures recognize that all human attainment must always be conditioned by the limitations that characterize man himself, but philosophy attempts to discover in nature and society some inevitable law of development that insures advance despite all the shortcomings of individuals. [4]

Sometimes history has been thought to exhibit an inescapable metaphysical principle of progression that

[4] This aspect of the philosophy of history has been surveyed at length by Troeltsch, *op. cit.*, pp. 221–693, and J. B. Bury, *The Idea of Progress: An Inquiry into Its Origin and Growth* (New York, 1921). The issue has frequently been discussed by sociologists—e.g., A. J. Todd, *Theories of Social Progress* (New York, 1918); L. M. Bristol, *Social Adaptation: A Study in the Development of the Doctrine of Adaptation as a Theory of Social Progress* (Cambridge, Massachusetts, 1915); Paul Barth, *Die Philosophie der Geschichte als Soziologie* (2d ed.; Leipzig, 1915); and appropriate sections in F. H. Hankins, "Sociology," in H. E. Barnes (ed.), *The History and Prospects of the Social Sciences* (New York, 1925), pp. 255–332, and C. A. Ellwood, *A History of Social Philosophy* (New York, 1938).

belongs to the very nature of the universe. Even the fact of social conflict has been interpreted as one of the main stimuli insuring development. Conflict brings into view the regnancy of the moral sense which is thought to reveal the inner drive of nature toward a higher life. Gradually men discover that at heart the universe is moral, and this knowledge will automatically insure the betterment of society. Or reliance may be placed more particularly upon man's capacity for intellectual growth. Just as nature is pervaded by a rational law that insures the coherence of phenomena, so, as man increasingly follows the light of reason, he rises to higher levels of attainment. Emancipated from error and enlightened by reason, he treads the pathway to perfectibility. This will be the inevitable outcome of intellectual advance through the increase of knowledge and the diffusion of education. Still others rely upon the logic of natural science. The laws of social evolution seem to them as dependable as the mechanistic operation of physical forces. Society, like all life in nature, is a struggle for adjustment to environment resulting in the survival of the fittest. Thus, nature herself has decreed that the best is yet to be.

On the other hand, the observational procedure does not seek to establish any metaphysical or natural law that will of itself render progress inevitable. Instead, it surveys the course of history to discover the specific respects in which advancement has become manifest. The point of departure is the most primitive state of civilization that appears on the distant horizon where the light of history first breaks in upon the scene. The slowly moving cycle of the centuries is followed through to the present moment, and from this perspective one may venture to forecast probabilities for the future. In this empirical pursuit the standard for measuring progress is the value which each successive generation attaches to its accomplishments over those of its predecessors. No ideally absolute norm is to be carried over from the past, and the future is left free to revise its standards of value in terms of its own tastes. One fallacy is to be strenuously avoided. The perennial restlessness of the human quest must never be shackled to any specific set of past or present estimates of worth. Evaluational opinions must be left as free to develop as is the historical process itself. Judgments of what is "good" and "better" and "best" are as fluid as is the stream of time.

The fact that the struggle for betterment refuses to come to rest at any particular stage of attainment is probably one of the chief reasons why some men lose faith in progress. They measure it in terms of fixity; and, when they discover that nothing stays permanently put in the constantly moving current of historical evolution, they drift into eddies of despair. They fail to realize that unceasing and strenuous effort is the price at which progress must always be purchased. This process involves not merely the activity of one or two generations of men, destined to be born and grow old and die within the narrow limits of six or seven decades, but the work of a ceaseless succession of new generations who possess the same recuperative powers and creative energy that have characterized their ancestors. The accumulations of civilization in the past must not be treated as endowments in perpetuity but as springboards from which to launch forth to fresh achievements in the future. There is no reason to suppose that the sources of vitality which have generated past and present attainments will not continue permanently in operation for ceaseless ages yet to come. Progress is in process of becoming; it has not yet arrived at any final goal. When this fact is appreciated, the story of civilization's achievements is prophetic of a better future and is not a harbor in which the voyagers on the sea of life come to permanent repose.

Viewing the course of civilization in its totality, no one can fail to perceive numerous evidences of progress. Who would choose to return if he could to the conditions of life that enveloped mankind in primitive times? Poverty is still a disagreeable fact, but its hold upon the human race is not to be compared with the penury of bygone days, when the struggle for food, clothing, and shelter occupied the total time and energies of men. The modern man's appetite would violently revolt against the fare upon which ordinary people were compelled to subsist even two centuries ago. The physical well-being of humanity still leaves much to be desired, but no perceiving person can fail to appreciate the progress that has been made in the production of food, the development of sanitation, provisions for medical care, improved housing conditions, and numerous material advantages that great numbers of people now enjoy beyond anything that their ancestors could imagine. Larger gains still await accomplishment, but the very fact of past advancements justifies the demand for further achievement and makes possible confidence in its realization. Progress itself inspires zeal for more progress and insures the prospect of its attainment.

The intellectual life exhibits a similar process of growth. Perhaps it is true, as some anthropologists have maintained, that in the latent capacities of his human brain the primitive man was fully the equal of moderns. The physical organism that generates thought may not have changed, but experience and discipline have certainly contributed to a remarkable development in the intellectual sphere. Our mental grasp of the world in which we live has grown to embrace a wealth of knowledge undreamed of by the ancients. Human intelligence comprehends the laws that hold the stars in their courses, reads the story of the earth's evolution during millenniums of time, and learns how to harness the latent forces of nature and control their power to heal man's ills or to drive his machines and serve his needs over an ever widening range of experience.

Technical skills have closely followed progress in knowledge. A Rip Van Winkle awakening today from a century of slumber would rub his eyes in stark amazement at what he would see. All about him he would witness men flying like birds in the air. Life in the home has been transformed by electrical devices for lighting, cooking, and heating. The telephone and the radio now bring to one's ears voices as from the dead. Public thoroughfares are crowded with vehicles impelled by invisible power from within. These things would have been unbelievable a few generations ago. Thousands of modern inventions have provided appliances for daily living that make it simply absurd for one to doubt progress in this area of experience. While it is true that technical advances may be used for good or for evil ends, to deny that they represent progress because they may be perverted is to judge them by a set of moral standards with which they themselves have nothing to do. It is not the person who produces the machine, but the one who uses it, who determines whether its service to humanity shall be good or bad. The machine itself bears eloquent testimony to the mechanical progress of man and is in no way responsible for his moral perversity.

At first glance, social progress may seem less certain. The problems involved are exceedingly complex, and mounting desires quickly outstrip attainments. Each step in advance opens up so many new vistas for further development that past accomplishments seem insignificant in comparison with future tasks. The more keenly awake one is to the need of social reforms, the less content is one with the situation today, however much it may excel that of yesterday. But if the history of social growth is viewed realistically, in terms of the actual developments of even the past century, no other area of civilization will exhibit clearer evidence of progress. This period has witnessed the abolition of slavery in the United States of America, the marvelous growth of our free public school system, the enactment of laws forbidding the exploitation of children in labor, legislation to insure the rights of workers in industry, provisions for the more humane treatment of criminals and the underprivileged, and a multitude of procedures rendering the world of human relations a more agreeable climate in which to live than had been known to men of any previous century. The farther one's vision penetrates into the past, the firmer becomes the conviction that society for the common man today exhibits amenities and opportunities such as he has never before been privileged to enjoy.

That history attests progressive development in man's political institutions cannot be so readily affirmed. From time to time recourse has been had to various types of organization, but none has proved in all respects ideal. From the days of Plato political philosophers have been legion; yet the practical operation of each system has left much to be desired. Today some nations idealize democracy, while others laud the virtues of imperial dictatorships. It is certainly true that in the political sphere progress lags far behind human attainments in other realms of culture. Particularly does the international scene still exhibit civilization at a primitively low level. Individuals and local communities have learned to live together without resort to violence, but rival nations have not, as yet, been able to shake off the blood lust of their brutal ancestors. Yet perhaps never before has the world been so keenly aware of its military depravity, and this awareness is itself a sign of progress in an area of civilization where advance has been far too long delayed. In the meantime some civic communities and national groups have reached the higher levels where political power is made to serve the ends of personal liberty and social justice. This is certainly a distinct advance; it reverses the older and once widely prevalent dictum that the citizen exists merely for the sake of the state.

Perhaps many persons will doubt whether history attests progress in the sphere of aesthetic, moral, and spiritual attainments. Did not the ancients write better poetry, paint more beautiful pictures, rear finer architectural monuments, compose more exquisite music, and live more saintly lives than do moderns? This is a subtle question that seems, in its very asking, to presuppose a negative answer. But one whose vision reaches far enough back in the stretches of time will have no hesitation in affirming that those several accomplishments were the result of a long previous process in cultural evolution. As records of human achievement they are landmarks of progress along the highway of history. Furthermore, when their uniqueness is recognized, we must not too quickly conclude that progress thereafter ceased. Sometimes new standards of excellence came into vogue and cultural diffusion supplanted individual distinction. The theory that every civilization is bound to decay as soon as it begins to penetrate the masses is open to grave doubt. Individuals may become less conspicuous while society in its totality rises to higher levels of achievement. The modern historian, whose vision embraces the totality of apprehensible time and the entire range of human activities, has no difficulty in persuading himself that never before have so many men been capable of aesthetic appreciation, moral idealism, and spiritual striving. And the surest guaranty of progress lies in the very fact that they are inspired, as never before, by a restless impulse toward still higher attainments.

D. THE PRACTICAL VALUE OF HUMAN HISTORY

The scientific quest for a knowledge of human history is not primarily concerned with the practical values to be derived from the results of research. Historians belonging to this school usually disclaim any ambition to formulate an abstract philosophy of history, and they question the propriety of elevating events or persons of the past to a position where they become idealized norms for all future ages. They abstain from passing judgment upon men or events. It is their business to portray in a purely objective manner exactly what took place; they refuse to express either approbation or censure. They would suppress all personal likes and dislikes and write neither to please readers nor to provide practical advice about conduct nor to arouse and direct emotions. Purely and simply to convey information is their professed intention.

If history is, at best, only an informative book of remembrance, is the labor required for its pursuit a wise expenditure of energy? To know the facts of the past would seem to be only a scholarly luxury unless this information contributes to effective living in the present. Since these historians divest the past of its providential and normative quality, the pursuit of their task might be thought a quite useless, or even a debasing, discipline. Nineteen hundred years ago Seneca pronounced history a harmful waste of time. He chided his contemporaries for their folly in narrating the deeds of monarchs and in recounting the cruelties and sufferings resulting from rival national ambitions. The vaunted war lords, like Philip of Macedon, Alexander the Great, and Hannibal, had been robbers of men, inspiring them to no higher ideal than to spend their lives in quest of a foe. It were better, far, to inquire about what ought to be done today than to recount the story of yesterday's evil deeds.

Seneca's skepticism has survived in some quarters even down to modern times. There are those who still think the study of history a useless pastime. They would forget the dead past and give themselves wholly to the solution of present and future problems. This attitude is a sensible one if history is thought to be only a mechanical recovery of fictitious norms for life today or is at best an assemblage of mortuary statistics. But that is a very superficial view of the subject. When we seek to recover the processes of life that produced history, we penetrate behind the dead facts to the vital scene in which the events transpired. We thereby widen our acquaintance with the actual people who have lived and worked in producing the kind of world in which we have been born and reared. Just as sociability and travel have an educative significance in broadening our acquaintance with contemporaries, so in the study of history we meet new people, share their life in other environments, and increase our capacity for understanding and pursuing the business of life today.

It is the historian only who can tell people how the given world in which they live has come to be what it is. When someone told Thomas Carlyle that George Eliot had decided to accept the universe, he is said to have remarked: "Gad, she'd better." Every living person is under the same necessity of accepting his universe; but, if he would understand how it has taken on its present character—physical, social, and cultural —he must acquaint himself with the processes of historical evolution. Only thus can he discover the genesis and function of social institutions, of prevailing customs and ideas, of current procedures in estimating values, and of the total range of phenomena that characterize contemporary civilization. It is history only that can make one intelligently at home in this inescapable world.

In so far as understanding can contribute to intelligent action, history may serve a useful purpose in

guiding present and future conduct. The probable outcome of a particular line of action may be foreseen in
the light of a given set of antecedents and consequents
that have often repeated themselves in the past. Procedures that have repeatedly proved futile in the course
of history may be avoided under the guidance of better
knowledge. The weight of a smothering tradition
may be borne with greater patience when the conditions that produced it and temporarily rendered it
functionally significant are fully comprehended. And
the task of altering a tradition will then be seen to in-
volve a process by which new functional values must
first emerge before new ways can be made to supplant
the old. Creative action is hedged about by hundreds
of conservative impedimenta that refuse to be brushed
aside until the causes which have produced and sustained them have been shown to be outmoded or in-
valid. When historical enlightenment is brought to
bear upon the situation, the path of progress is more
easily cleared of obstructions.

Perhaps the outstanding value of history, when
viewed as the long record of human activity, is a new
sense of man's responsibility for creating a better society. Man makes his own world of culture; civilization is the product of his ideals and activities. The
biological doctrine of the survival of the fittest does
not carry the same force in history as in physical science, because there is always the unpredictable factor
of man's power to choose his course of action. His desires, his emotions, his imagination, his likes or dis-

likes, and his rational judgments operate to shape and confuse the outcome of his living. He sometimes learns by experience, but he often acts on impulse. Only by strenuous self-discipline can he accustom himself to do that which is good for his individual and social health. The best will not prevail unless his initiative and judgment are consciously controlled in the interests of worthy ends. And in this task history is one of his most reliable tutors.

This principle applies throughout the entire range of human conduct. In no sphere of culture will man's attainments rise above the level of his most strenuous endeavors. It has always been so in the past and apparently will continue to be so for all future time. Popular acclaim for outstanding accomplishments in art, literature, philosophy, science, or religion commonly ignores the background of persistent and devoted efforts that have conditioned ultimate success. When a friend commented approvingly on one of Tennyson's lines in which the diction seemed a stroke of genius, the poet confessed that the final word of the line had cost him three cigars. Attainment is the sequel to persistent striving. Even in the religious firmament, those whose stars shine brightest were seasoned toilers at their tasks.

The human view of history seeks to portray the story of the past as a vital process of man's endeavor in every area of his activity. His mistakes and his successes are integral parts of the picture, and both have their educational value for everyone who reads the story. The total presentation tells moderns how their world has come into existence and assigns to them the task of determining its future. Strenuous activism is held up to view as the only program that will insure success. The future will be exactly what men make of it, whether they strive merely in their own strength or seek divine guidance for their endeavors. In either event the full responsibility rests with them. Genius will never consent to serve as a substitute for honest toil, and God will never risk his cause in the hands of an indolent devotee.

CHAPTER IV

THE REVIVAL OF HISTORICAL DUALISM

AT THE opening of the twentieth century, historical thinking seemed to have become a permanent characteristic of the intellectual life. The present status of the world was assumed to be the result of a gradual process of growth; everything was to be understood in terms of historical development. In the physical realm, evolution explained how star dust had issued in an orderly cosmos, how the earth had changed from a molten mass into a habitable globe, and how life, springing from a single cell, had culminated in a multiplicity of species. By slow stages cultural life had emerged from a state of primitivity until it had assumed its present complex forms. The mind of man had gradually learned how to master itself and control its environment. Social institutions had arisen and taken on diversity of form in response to emerging needs. Even religion was viewed in the light of a developmental process, the successive stages of which were capable of being understood only in terms of historical growth. The whole of civilization represented a progressive movement of expansion surely advancing, either directly or in zigzag fashion, toward higher levels of achievement.

A strongly reactionary type of thinking has come

into prominence during more recent decades. It casts grave doubts upon the unity and continuity of the historical process. Emphasis is placed upon the conflicts and unresolved contradictions in nature and cultural life. Good and evil are said to exist side by side in a perpetual struggle wherein neither attains final victory. The motivations of mankind, taken as a whole, are vacillating and inharmonious; they lack driving power toward one ideal goal. Economic life is pervaded by an interminable battle between rival interests. International relations breed war rather than comity. Intellectuals may profess allegiance to rationality and yet fight bitterly over contrary opinions. The whole world is one vast arena of embattled opposites, and its ultimate nature is incapable of being understood by the unifying hypothesis of progressive historical development. Its secret can be discovered only by recognizing the fact of irreconcilable contradictions, by setting up against every affirmation its corresponding negation, by admitting the necessity of dealing constantly with pros and cons, and by refusing to be deluded into believing that the conflict can ever be resolved upon the plane of mundane existence. This procedure is known as the "dialectical" method, or the philosophy of "crisis." When applied to the interpretation of history, it has produced what may be called the "cult of crisis," propounded to offset what its devotees have scornfully termed the "cult of progress."

[93]

A. THE CULT OF CRISIS

The dialectical mind is not primarily interested in history. For the dialectician the important moment is the present, which brings one to full consciousness of the conflict between opposites and the awareness of their irreconcilability. All of life is pervaded by contradictions. Heat and cold, light and darkness, life and death, love and hate, hope and despair, are illustrations of phenomena that refuse to be synthesized. Both prevail, and there is no substantial middle ground between them where humanity may come to rest. It is as if men were riding upon a perpetual seesaw where equilibrium is unattainable. It is not necessary to seek confirmation of this fact from history, since present experience sufficiently attests its truth. This knowledge is derived from the immediacy of the "existential" moment which reveals the real self and its inability to escape the dilemma. The "crisis" must be endured; it cannot be resolved, because it is integral to all human living on the terrestrial plane. There can be no change in this situation until time has ceased and eternity has dawned. Hence, it is utterly futile to search temporal history for a solution of the problem.

It is the custom nowadays to make the Danish philosopher Sören Kierkegaard the father of the "dialectical" method of reasoning. He lived largely unnoticed in the first half of the nineteenth century; but early in the next century German scholars studied and translated his writings, and more recently these have been introduced to English readers.[1]

It is not difficult to understand Kierkegaard's type of thinking when it is viewed in the light of his peculiar personality and contemporary situation. Following the Napoleonic wars, Denmark experienced social conditions that fostered a philosophy of despair by a thinker whose temperament did not fit him for aggressive action on the stage of practical life. He was an individualist unable to integrate himself with the situation in his external world. He always sensed a wide gulf between himself and society and lived constantly, as he himself affirms, on the verge of melancholia. His sensitive and high-strung nature kept his emotions at white heat. He had a frail body and sought in strenuous mental activity to compensate for his lack of physical power. The gloomy Christian piety that he had inherited from his father grew more intense as he meditated upon his unhappy situation and the failure of institutional Christianity, as it was current in Denmark, to relieve his distress. Hence, he exalted to the place of supremacy in religion the notion of the sharp contrast between man's imperfection and the absolute righteousness of God. Confronted by

[1] For example, *Philosophical Fragments*, translated by David F. Swenson; *Stages on Life's Way*, translated by Walter Lowrie; *Concluding Unscientific Postscript*, translated by David F. Swenson and Walter Lowrie; and *Sickness unto Death*, translated by Walter Lowrie, have recently been published by the Princeton University Press. A good brief introduction to Kierkegaard is E. L. Allen, *Kierkegaard: His Life and Thought* (New York, 1936); see also Walter Lowrie, *Kierkegaard* (New York, 1938).

the Divine Absolute, the truly religious person should become aware of his complete bankruptcy and utter worthlessness. This is the crisis from which there is no escape in this world. But one who has arrived at this state of mind can become genuinely religious by trusting solely in God and eternity for the hope of ultimate salvation. Complete terrestrial pessimism is the key to celestial optimism.

This Christian philosophy of despair consigned history to the cosmic rubbish heap. To suppose that the Kingdom of God would ever be a temporal establishment was absurd; it belonged only to eternity. The Hegelian notion that the divine idea was gradually coming to realization through the struggling process of human living on earth was ridiculous. When man pursued this way of thinking, he was committing the cardinal sin of egoistic self-esteem. He had forgotten his utter worthlessness before the absolute God. On his own initiative and by his puny efforts man could do nothing except go astray and fall into sin. To imagine that he could participate constructively in any work of God, or was competent to "think God's thoughts after him," was the height of sinful human pride. For Kierkegaard, as for Hegel, God was the transcendental absolute; but Kierkegaard would not allow the Deity to become immanently entangled in human history. He stood wholly outside the historical process and was to be apprehended by men only as they mounted on the wings of faith from the valley of time to the invisible heights of eternity.

It follows that the idea of progress in history is absolutely untenable. History is moving neither up nor down; it is going nowhere and is without directive guidance by either God or man. Accidental events in time have no logical or essential connection with the reality of infinity. Time neither originates nor culminates in eternity but is a meaningless interlude in which men momentarily exist in order to accomplish nothing of importance except the attainment of a state of mind. They discover that they stand helplessly before God, upon whom they depend for salvation in the eternal life to come. Present social activism directed toward the realization of religious ideals on the human level is a misguided effort. It may, indeed, be positively harmful in that it obscures the consciousness of crisis and dulls the sense of despair which alone can teach man his impotence in the presence of God. Thus only can man appreciate the importance of abandoning all trust in his worthless self and come to a full realization of his helplessness in the presence of absolute perfection. The divine standard is so utterly beyond the attainment of man that attempts to approximate it by historical efforts to implement a better way of life on earth simply add to the mounting sin of self-reliance and pride. When men assume to be fellow-workers with God, they are guilty of sacrilegious self-esteem.

Karl Barth's espousal of the doctrine of crisis, restated in terms of traditional Calvinism, has attracted wide attention since the close of the first World War, in the year 1918. It has won numerous adherents on the Continent of Europe, in the British Isles, and in the United States of America.[2]

The result of the Barthian movement has been a decline of interest in the human processes of history and the reassertion of a dualistic way of thinking that relegates religion to the sphere of the suprahistorical. Religion is no longer envisaged as a human attainment in man's struggle to apprehend and perform the divine will. Rather, it is a donation from the outer world of eternity, a supernaturally mediated revelation, that has impinged upon the temporal world. Men accomplish their salvation by passively accepting the divine decrees, not by growing in historical righteousness. The underlying postulates of this type of thinking allow no place for the self-revelation of God in the area of human experience, nor is his kingdom to be realized by any progress in historical evolution. Time and eternity are two distinct and antagonistic entities. In the former, men experience only crisis, from which there is no release in the present world.

God's participation in human history is excluded by

[2] For an introduction to the Barthian type of thinking one may consult Wilhelm Pauck, *Karl Barth, Prophet of a New Christianity?* (New York, 1931); Walter Lowrie, *Our Concern with the Theology of Crisis* (Boston, 1932); E. G. Homrighausen, *Christianity in America: A Crisis* (New York, 1936); E. E. Aubrey, *Present Theological Tendencies* (New York, 1936), pp. 55–112. Books by Barth available in English are: *The Word of God and the Word of Man* (Boston, 1928); *The Epistle to the Romans* (London, 1933); *The Doctrine of the Word of God* (New York, 1936); *Credo* (New York, 1937); *The Knowledge of God and the Word of God* (New York, 1939); *This Christian Cause* (New York, 1941).

the notion of his total "otherness." He is in no way involved in the processes of the material universe, although it has been created and is sustained by him. But in spiritual affairs he stands completely aloof from and above the mundane order. He is accessible neither in the orderly processes of nature nor in the rational operations of the human mind nor in the moral idealism of mankind. In no respect is he immanent in the created world of men and things. He is beyond the reach of the natural man, and yet he is the inexorable judge whom all men face in their helplessness. Although he does not mingle with them in their mundane affairs, he is the only source from which they can derive salvation. This is to be insured by faith, as they recognize his unapproachable holiness and abandon hope of ever being able to meet his righteous demands. They perform his will, not by striving to bring his kingdom to fulfilment among men, but by realizing their utter inability to perform anything pleasing in his sight. On the stage of history there is no reward for virtuous human effort.

Another reason for neglecting history is the doctrine of man's helplessness and total depravity. By blind impulse and false opinions humans are deluded into believing that they can perform good deeds. They vainly imagine that by seeking they can find God and by worthy living can win his approval. They strive to generate righteousness of which God only is the source. Their best intentions and most strenuous efforts are but "filthy rags" in his sight. Their institutional programs for improvement of character and social betterment are sheer mockery from the divine point of view. Goodness must always be God's gift; it can never be man's achievement. On the natural level of human history men move like puppets on a stage manipulated by their own devices that are arrogantly assumed to be divine decrees. True men of God do not rise up to action but repose in despair of their own powers and wait for God to bring an end to time and usher in eternity.

Through revelation only can divine help come to mankind. But this does not come by a gradual process in which light breaks through to the human spirit at successive levels of attainment in religious living. Men do not grasp revelation from within the process of spiritual striving and achievement on the historical plane; it is superimposed from above by God himself. It is not a process but a sporadic and supernatural act. God speaks, and man hears. Nor is this message a didactic communication to guide the devout in daily living. Rather, it is the negation of all natural aspirations and powers by the affirmation of God's transcendence and unapproachable righteousness. Before this utterance every man stands condemned and confounded; he humbly accepts the crisis, and divine approval is his reward. He is then on the road to salvation. He is not freed from the critical paradoxes in which all human living is involved, but he has heard the Word of God and waits upon the divine good pleasure. But if, at any moment, man takes matters into his own hands and tries to shape history in conformity with his ideals, however noble they may be, he forfeits the right to God's approval and courts disaster.

This philosophy of despair regarding the present world order was excellently adapted to the mental status of post-war Europe, particularly in Germany. Past history had been blotted out of memory by the tragedy of more recent events. If faith in God was to survive, his chief domain of activity had to be assigned to the transcendental sphere. History on the terrestrial plane seemed to have been an unhappy interregnum in the supernatural government of the universe. God stood aloof from human affairs, save as he towered above them in judgment and summoned men to a realization of their own helplessness. Their efforts in the past to erect a stable and prosperous civilization seemed to have come to naught. Apparently it had been a mistake to assume that God had sponsored so futile an undertaking. Now one could see that the Deity had not been immanently active in the making of the human enterprise but stood totally aloof from its vanities. Sacred and secular history were separate processes moving in distinctive orbits whose points of intersection were moments of revelation. Taken as a whole, history was a duality of human and divine action—the one terrestrial, temporal, and aimless; the other celestial, eternal, and infinitely wise. And one who would understand the ultimate meaning of history must seek it in the sphere of transcendentalism.

B. DIALECTICAL EXPONENTS OF HISTORICAL DUALISM

In general, the disciples of dialectical thinking and the advocates of crisis theology have not concerned themselves especially with history. But there have been a few exceptions, notably Nicolas Berdyaev,[3] Paul Tillich,[4] and Otto Piper.[5] Each has attempted, in a distinctive way, to show that history is a dual entity shaped by one type of forces on the mundane level and by a different set of influences in the metaphysical sphere.

Berdyaev reads the meaning of the total course of history under the magnifying glass of calamities experienced by the Russian Orthodox church as a result of the Bolshevik Revolution, which ultimately forced the author into exile. His book is a translation of lectures delivered in Moscow at the Liberal Academy of Spiritual Culture in 1919–20, but its interpretation of history would not need to be essentially altered by the use of illustrative materials drawn from the events of the two subsequent decades. Quite naturally, in conformity with his personal and social experience, he resorts to eschatology for the pattern of his historical thinking. Temporal history is only the story of conflict and tragedy which can be brought to a happy end solely by a divine intervention that inaugurates a new world order. Then calamitous "terrestrial" history

[3] *The Meaning of History* (New York, 1936).

[4] *The Interpretation of History* (New York, 1936), and in the Oxford Conference Book, *The Kingdom of God and History* (Chicago, 1938), pp. 107–41.

[5] *God in History* (New York, 1939).

will be swallowed up in triumphant "celestial" history. Thus, one is optimistic as to the ultimate outcome while thoroughly pessimistic about the nature of the temporal process.

Yet the tragic element in history is present in both its celestial and its terrestrial career. Human suffering, as exhibited in history, reflects the element of suffering that is resident in the very heart of God. The evidence that conflict and tragedy belong to the interior nature of God, as well as to the historic career of man, is found in the traditional Christian doctrine of the incarnation. This is the symbol, or indeed the reality, exhibiting the true spiritual dynamism of God breaking through into the material world to share with fallen man the tragedies of his existence. The passion and sufferings of the Son of God reveal the inner nature of the Supreme Deity and thus disclose the character of metaphysical reality. The coming of Christ bridged the chasm between the metaphysical and the historical; in him they became united and identified. The end toward which this process moves is eternal destiny at the close of time; it is an eschatological reality to be supernaturally revealed.

Berdyaev provides for man's role in the making of history by affirming the doctrine of human freedom. This is not a freedom to determine the course of events but is a creative responsibility for choosing between spiritual and material ends. The natural man's alienation from the spirit of God, his immersion in elemental nature, and his sense of bondage to fate had shackled his creative spiritual powers until the revelation in Christ restored the divine image in man and reinvested him with his lost divine sonship. Thus, in Christianity a new era of history was inaugurated wherein man became a free subject who waged war on the natural elements both within and outside of himself. But he does not look for final victory under the limits of time. To attempt this type of success would mean re-enslavement to temporal and natural powers. The struggle between the natural and the spiritual must always result in tragedy during the present eon. The inevitable failure of terrestrial history is the surest attestation of the higher calling and superhistorical destiny of mankind. The true progress and goal of human endeavor can be correctly apprehended only in terms of transcendental eschatology.

A more rigorous application of dialectic to the interpretation of history has been advanced by Tillich. His book brings together in English translation an epitome of different treatises that had appeared in German during the decade prior to the year 1933. Happily, an autobiographical sketch has been prefixed to the collection. In this the author indicates the personal experiences and the historical occurrences that have been influential in shaping his thinking. He openly affirms that he has reared his philosophy of history upon the basis of reality as experienced in the crises and catastrophes of the last three decades in middle Europe. The experience is doubly real for him in that he not only participated actively in life within

Germany during those crucial days but has now been forced into exile as a member of that German intellectual dispersion whose social and religious views proved displeasing to the Hitler regime. American readers, who have not shared the author's background and fate, may have difficulty in accepting the interpretation here presented. They do not find it ringing true to the actualities of their "existential" situation, or at least not until the situation has been cut to fit the foreign pattern. But Tillich does not attempt this task; he abides strictly by the European scene.

History is interpreted in terms of three categories: the philosophical, the political, and the theological. From the philosophical standpoint, existence is defined by the use of a dual imagery of the conditioned and the Unconditioned (the word is to be capitalized). The latter is not, however, separable in time or action from the conditioned. The two are in a constant state of interaction, and the latter perpetually discloses the former. Temporal phenomena are always attended by tension, struggle, tragedy, and uncertainty, from which there is no final escape in concrete history. One must resort to metaphysics for the explanation of this situation. The experience of perplexity and crisis is thought to attest the existence of a basal metaphysical reality of inexhaustible, formless, and absolute being which man's historical experiences vaguely but positively disclose, although human thinking and logic cannot penetrate this mystery. It is known ultimately and truly only by intuition. Yet the essential truth is the same whether the experience serves to blind or to clarify our vision into the mysterious depths of the inexhaustible. The important fact for understanding its meaning is an awareness of the "abyss," from which we too often falsely endeavor to divorce history.

By defining the relation between the metaphysical absolute and finite existences in dynamic, rather than static, imagery, Tillich allows a place for human free will and responsibility in the making of history. There is said to be a perpetual force emanating from the "abyss," a dynamic that is mightily disturbing but never supernaturally directive, that is constantly form-creating and form-destroying, called by the author the "demonic." This is not to be identified with the popular notion of the satanic, nor with the primitive conception of spirits, whether good or bad. Rather, it is a kind of impersonal cosmic urge breaking through from behind concrete existence to disturb constantly its equilibrium. This "demonic" force is not opposed to the divine, as though a fierce conflict was being waged from above between two hostile powers. But it sets the stage for human decision. It is the genius of the demonic to be concerned with form and of the divine to be concerned with inexhaustible unity of being. Man is demonic when engaged in the effort to give permanent validity to forms of political, social, or religious institutions or when he takes upon himself the responsibility for delimiting or defining God. God is thereby "demonized." What man should do, if he would be in accord with the divine and escape the

[106]

"demonic," is to surrender to the Unconditioned, even though he perceives that it judges, destroys, and breaks him. He must be content to live in crisis.

History acquires absolute meaning, whether cultural or political or religious, only when viewed in terms of the divine demonic imagery. Thus, history takes on a truly transcendental character reaching both backward and forward into eternity. The terrestrial scene is only an interlude filled with conflict, agony, and despair. Thus man, buffeted by transitory phenomena which he vainly tries to shape and control, is driven to the realization of his own futility in the presence of the divine judgment. Perceiving that the battle of the divine against the "demonic" cannot be won by works but is ultimately a matter of grace by which alone salvation is obtainable, man resigns himself in faith to the mysterious Unconditioned that has to be sensed by intuition as the metaphysical basis of the total complexity of existential phenomena. Action on man's part is still obligatory in order that he may keep alive and enlarge his consciousness of the divine, but activity becomes "demonized" when it is directed toward the establishment of would-be authoritative institutions, whether they be social or political or religious, designed to effect salvation on the terrestrial plane. This consummation belongs not to time but to eternity. It is eschatological; it falls beyond time. Thus the pessimistic story of temporal history is transfigured and transcendentalized by the magic of metaphysical dialectic.

Piper's dichotomy of history is less involved. He would concede that God makes history, but he would assign man no function in bringing the divine purposes to realization. History is thought to exhibit two distinct phases, the secular and the sacred. With the latter only is God essentially concerned. The providential view of Augustine is reaffirmed in the temper of Calvinistic theology and rephrased in terms of the doctrine of crisis inspired by recent happenings in Europe. The modern methodology of the secular historian has no pertinence to the problem of recovering more accurately the story of religious history.

Secular history is simply Satan's business, while religious history is the story of God's supernatural intervention in mundane affairs as recorded in the biblical revelation. It began more particularly with the call of Abraham; it was perpetuated in the work of a long line of inspired prophets in Israel; and it culminated when Jesus entered the world, miraculously born of a virgin. It is futile to suppose that by scientific research into the nature of the world and man one can hope to find God and better understand his relations with the world. Outside of the Bible, there is no revelation of God worthy of quest. The birth of Jesus was the climactic emergence of God in history, and since that date there has been a gradual veiling of his presence by the prevalent disposition of the church to come to terms with the secular world. The attempt of Christians to establish the Kingdom of God on earth by making socially effective the ideals of Christian teaching is a misguided effort. The truly religious man should be more concerned about what God can do for him and less busy trying to work in the world on behalf of God by means of social programs for improvement or by building up ecclesiastical institutions to serve on the human level. Secular history cannot be improved by these devices of men. In fact, God does not wish to have it improved, since it is due for destruction rather than redemption. The present state of affairs will endure—how long no one knows—until the catastrophic intervention of Christ to bring the evil world to an end and establish the Kingdom of God in its perfection.

This interpretation of history is readily understood when we recall the unhappy circumstances of the author. He is now an exile from his native land, forced out by Nazi persecution. The poignancy of the situation in Germany seems to give to this particular segment of history a distinctly cosmic significance. The long ages that have preceded, and the countless centuries that are to follow, fade into oblivion under the scorching light of the immediate scene. The illimitable reaches of time are blotted out of the picture, and a foreshortened view of history results. The apparent and temporary futility of human effort to institute remedial measures is translated into permanent defeat, and faith can survive only by resort to the Barthian doctrine of crisis supplemented by a revival of ancient Christian millenarianism. What we really have here is not an exposition of God in history but the affirma-

tion of a specific type of faith in God to support one
when passing through a particularly trying experience.

C. MILDER FORMS OF HISTORICAL DUALISM

The disposition to disparage man's part in the making of history has led to various attempts to discover
other sets of forces whose operation is thought to have
been inadequately recognized. In this procedure, also,
the totality of the historical process is conceived not
as a unity but as a duality of discordant forces striving
for supremacy. Moreover, the human urge that has
thus far dominated in the making of civilization is
thought to have gone astray. The hope for improvement lies in recognizing and giving right of way to
some heretofore suppressed influence or idea that alone
is competent to correct the unhappy status of modern
society.

A few years ago Gerald Heard completed a series of
studies[6] in which he sought to show the secret of
civilization's failure and to define the basis on which
future success might be insured. Finally he believed he
had discovered the key to a solution of all the problems that trouble the modern social order. As he views
the matter, the central evil which afflicts the world
today is its war mania. This disease is thought to be
the culmination of a long series of perverted assumptions emanating from the erroneous belief that conscious individuals can create a worthy social order.
The remedy proposed is that human behavior should

[6] *The Source of Civilization* (New York, 1937).

[110]

be left to the control of forces to be discovered "below the level of consciousness." Apparently history, when worthily made by men, must be the product of their subconscious living.

Natural science, archeology, and history are extensively explored in defense of the author's thesis. In each of these areas he finds what he believes to be ample evidence that human thinking and endeavor have thus far been on the wrong track. He vigorously condemns the doctrine of the survival of the fittest in biological evolution and would displace it by the survival value of a pervasive subconscious sensitivity or awareness of life's meaning. Yet he has to admit that such sensitivity readily induces a conscious effort which, on the author's hypothesis, inevitably leads to struggle, conflict, and ultimate disaster. Every conscious effort of man to improve his status in the world leads automatically to the nullification of his purpose. It is man's capacity to "feel," rather than to attain values by conscious effort, that provides the only solid foundation for a happy social existence.

The historical civilizations that have arisen at different centers in the past are believed to have crumbled because of deliberate efforts to maintain themselves against real or imaginary hostile forces. This fact is found to have been true not only of political and social institutions but also of religious organizations. Only in India does any ray of light penetrate the prevailing darkness that envelops the history of our so-called "civilization." The Yoga philosophy, in its psychological attempt to grasp the reality of extra-individuality and an "awareness of its subconscious linkage with all Life and Being," caught a glimpse of the truth. But, even so, it did not successfully prevent the rise of an acute individualism in historic Indian culture. This task remains to be accomplished in the modern world, and on the success of this endeavor depends the rise of a true civilization and the eventual emergence of a new form of history.

One cannot fail to admire Heard's evangelistic zeal in condemning the all too prevalent supposition that civilization can be built on a program of violence, however much the doctrine may be refined by political or religious sanctions. But to discard individual human effort directed by the highest conscious ideals that man is able to cultivate, and instead to trust our fate to the vague promptings of subconscious mental life, hardly seems to offer the promise of stability that we need. Its directive power is too uncertain and evanescent to enlarge our sense of brotherhood and lift us above the menace of individual, racial, and national selfishness. Not until the realm of the subconscious has been invested with a kind of supernatural authority or has been converted into a sublimated moral and ethical idealism would this "unconscious relation with the inner world" seem to acquire the prestige demanded of it in this connection. Any making of human history that is not the product of man's conscious effort to produce a better world must assign the processes of history to an order of existence lying outside the range of ordinary experience. This dualism of conscious and subconscious life would thus imply not one but two histories.

A similar type of interpretation has been advanced by John Macmurray,[7] who finds the ordinary processes of history to have been a perversion of the divine intention that is still waiting for realization in the new history to be made in the future. Instead of Heard's appeal to the unconscious as the new directive force, Macmurray finds it in an ideal social activism. The fundamental defect in our modern culture is the separation between rational thinking and practical activity. When rationalization precedes action, the outcome of effort is always to produce exactly the opposite result from that designed. A healthful society cannot be derived from the rational ideal of reformers but must be a realization in action. Unity is possible only where there is continuity of intentional activity. This thesis is found to have been the very genius of the Jewish consciousness and the essence of Christianity as set forth by Jesus. It is this observation that gives one the clue to history.

Jesus is said to have been the exponent of the notion that reality is only to be found in action. He did not advocate an ideal of how life ought to be lived, but he exemplified a program of intentional procedure. Hence, Christianity is to be defined as the "continuity of an intention incorporated in practice." It is not to be conceived of as a varied and developing religious

[7] *The Clue to History* (New York, 1939).

movement that has been in process of growth for nineteen hundred years. On the contrary, it is an original proposition enunciated by Jesus and almost immediately blurred or completely obscured by his later disciples until recently recovered by Macmurray's social theory to the effect that intentional activity, rather than rational reflection, is the motive power that creates worthy history.

The content of Jesus' intention is therefore a matter of prime importance. It first emerged in history as the experience of the Hebrew people. They avoided the mistake of the Greeks in exalting the notion of the reflective life, and they shunned the Roman error of stressing the practical institutions of social organization. Instead, they integrated action and reflection in the area of religion, and thus they were the first to apprehend truly the purpose of God in history. In Jesus the processes of Jewish history reached completion and were defined in terms of finality. It is a mistake to suppose that Jesus was either a social reformer or a teacher of ideals; he was both and more. Above everything else, he was the exponent of a life of action which gave expression in its purest form to God's intention that human history should not be a dualism of two worlds—one good and one evil, in eternal conflict with one another—but a single world in which by a life of action the supreme purpose of God in the creation of man was to realize a community of free and equal persons.

It follows that Jesus has been sadly misunderstood

for some nineteen hundred years. The European branches of Christendom were not Christianity at all, and yet Christianity survived within Roman and medieval society by virtue of the fact that it was the source of a pressure which the church constantly resisted but was able neither to eject nor to absorb. This constant pressure was the underlying purpose of God in history to have men create in action a communal society in accordance with the principles of the Kingdom as they had been expounded by Jesus. Thus, true Christianity had survived as a divine intention impelling co-operative action to create a new form of society in which equality, freedom, and common humanity would be realized. But this realization had been continually thwarted by the rise of ecclesiastical authority, the emergence of the economic struggle, and the dualistic procedure of separating between thought and action. Only in modern times has Russian communism begun a new chapter in the history of the Christian intention, but thus far Russia has made the sad mistake of failing to realize that its action is in accord with God's purposes as revealed in Hebrew history and stated in final form by Jesus.

The explanation proposed by Macmurray obliterates from Hebrew history the national consciousness of a distinctive and chosen race. Also, it ignores the sense of bitter conflict between the Kingdom of Satan and the Kingdom of God that permeated the thinking of Jesus and inspired the vivid eschatological hopes of early Christianity. Moreover, we are still left with

[115]

two histories—one marking the course of human perversity in thinking and the other disclosing a divinely revealed program of activity represented by Jesus but as yet only feebly pursued by mankind. History is not a progressive sequence of events but a conflict between the ignorant designs of men and the operation of a divine intention revealed by Jesus.

Charles Harold Dodd[8] has reverted to an outright theological interpretation of history. He revives the old distinction between secular and sacred history and sees in the latter the true significance of temporal events. Secular history is largely meaningless, but sacred history is that series of occurrences in which Jews and Christians have believed themselves able to detect the self-revealing activity of God. The process began with the call of Abraham and culminated in the emergence of the church. The end of the development was reached in the life, death, and resurrection of Jesus Christ and the institution of the Eucharist. Henceforth sacred history knows no further evolution. While the church as an institution partakes of the character of secular history, its ultimate function is simply to proclaim the unique event that happened once for all with the coming of Christ to earth. The business of the church is to announce this final intervention of God in history and to visualize the presence

[8] *History and the Gospel* (New York, 1938); also his essay in H. G. Wood and Others, *The Kingdom of God and History* (Chicago, 1938). All of the essays in the latter volume, with the single exception of E. W. Lyman's, move in the orbit of the traditional dichotomy of secular-sacred history or in the realm of Barthian transcendentalism.

of Christ in the Eucharist, where sacred history reached its climax nineteen centuries ago.

Thus there are two histories, one pertaining to the succession of events in time and the other being an insert from God out of eternity. The former is incapable of yielding any significant meaning; one cannot say whether its course is marked by progress or by deterioration. It is merely a series of happenings that has in view no goal. Sacred history, on the other hand, partakes of the nature of eternity impinging upon time through Christ and the church. The resurrection of Jesus marked its climactic manifestation, but in the history of the church it continues to function as judgment and mercy operating on the terrestrial level. Yet the success of the church is not to be insured by any program of human effort; one may not posit a final victory for goodness within the span allotted to the life of mankind on earth. Here the influence of Barth is in evidence. Only by the entry into history of a reality from beyond history—by a creative act of God vertically from above—must history finally be judged. In some vague way secular history will finally be supplanted by sacred history as the Kingdom of God eventuates in eternity. When or how this consummation will be realized remains, as yet, unknown.

D. INCENTIVES FOR HISTORICAL DUALISM

All dualistic conceptions of history create for themselves some artificial metaphysical theory that takes priority over concrete events belonging to the temporal scene. Either a hypothetically determined meaning is read into historical incidents or else they are denied the very possibility of meaning. It has to be superimposed from without—if, indeed, it is not an absolute reversal of those values that inhere in observable historical phenomena. The key to the understanding of history on the terrestrial plane is not to be sought in the sequence and momentum of events that belong strictly to the process of time. The task demands a more esoteric type of wisdom. One must have eyes capable of penetrating behind the veil of actual events in order to discover, by resort to some metaphysical hypothesis, the secrets of the superearthly history which reveals the meaning of, or is destined to supplant outright, the totality of current temporal happenings.

In the last analysis the dualistic interpretation of history is designed to provide a mechanism of escape from the stern realities of human existence. The increasing complexity of the modern world has tremendously enlarged man's responsibilities for maintaining the health of the social order. But the enormity of the task seems to place it beyond his powers of accomplishment. Faith in the triumph of justice and righteousness needs some stronger support than is furnished by past records of human effort in the world of historical reality. Presently the awareness of calamities becomes so acute that the attempts of men to prevent disaster seem futile. The temporal scene thus loses significance, and pious imagination constructs a supratemporal world whither the perplexed may flee for the solution of life's unresolved problems. Since terrestrial history is believed to hold in store no promise of ultimate betterment, celestial history is imaginatively constructed to eliminate all possibility of defeat. It becomes a longed-for harbor of safety for the troubled spirits of men. What they cannot do for themselves, even with all the divine assistance at present available, God will triumphantly effect for them in the eternal future.

The motives that have induced the skeptical attitude toward the present world are easy to understand. The last half-century has been a period of rapid and radical change. Many ordinary human procedures have gone awry. Old ways have been rudely dislocated, and new ones have been slow to gain recognition. A century or two is a relatively brief period in the evolution of world culture, but to the individual who participates in the events of the period the life of his generation may seem to mark the end of an era. Abandoning any hope for betterment in his lifetime, he makes the totality of terrestrial history simply a replica of his individual experience. Since he can visualize no attainment of personal satisfaction amid the distresses of the contemporary scene, the entire course of history falls under the shadow of his pessimism. He fails to note that the death agonies of each old stage in the evolution of civilization are also the birth pangs of a new age.

In order to justify one's lack of faith in the processes

of terrestrial history, attention is centered upon its defects and calamities. These things are assumed to be its normal products, while the attainment of moral and spiritual ideals either is denied or is credited to some extraneous divine operation that is said to impinge upon the world from without. No inherent trend toward goodness can be allowed a place in the normal order of existence. Even though it be admitted that the present world has been created by God, no divine power is allowed to remain present and operative in the processes of terrestrial history. God cannot be permitted any intimate association with a course of events that is thought to be characterized by disaster, distress, and decadence. The more emphatically the shadows in the picture are magnified, the more convinced does the artist become that the Deity is not actively engaged in the making of human history. But it is held to be inconceivable that God should not be concerned about men who have been created in his image. Hence, an extra-worldly history is hypothecated to furnish the stage upon which God and man may re-establish normal relations. Since this privilege is denied them in the present order of being, the incentive for positing its supramundane reality becomes doubly imperative.

Not only is God doing nothing to improve world history, but man himself should realize that he is incapable of effecting advancement. All of his attempts are declared to be futile. This affirmation is supported by selecting as typical the darkest spots marking human failures within the historical panorama. Since, for example, many institutions established by men have collapsed, does not that fact prove human incompetence to build an effective civilization? One forgets to note that the demise of an old institution is only a progressive step toward the growth of some new and more efficient establishment. But, since healthful development is, by hypothesis, denied to history, one laments the passing of the deceased and pays no regard to the future possibilities of the newly born. The dark hour through which one is momentarily passing casts its sinister shadow over the remotest regions of both the past and the future.

Furthermore, it is alleged that man himself is totally incapable of making successful history. The natural man is utterly depraved; and the redeemed man ought to realize that, even though he remains in the world, it is no longer an integral factor in his existence. He assumes for himself quite too much dignity when he supposes that he has been intrusted with the responsibility for establishing God's kingdom upon earth. This perverse notion is said to be the result of a misguided and sinful ambition. To assign man this role would mean that human history, having become God's concern, might grow better and better from age to age. Since this possibility must be denied in order to maintain the worthlessness of temporal history, man cannot be allowed any capacity for creative goodness in world affairs. The value of his past accomplishments is disparaged or ignored; his evil impulses and perverted activities are stressed; progressive improvement attending his efforts is stoutly denied; and the cultural development of the human race from the days of primitivity to modern times fails to make any impression upon these pessimistic interpreters of history.

It is also assumed that God himself has lost faith in men as makers of history. Consequently, he acts independently of men, and thus sacred history is to be sharply differentiated from secular. The latter is pervaded by blind accident; it lacks positive drive toward a clearly envisaged goal; and it is without any authoritative supervision. Although the Deity stands in judgment over human history, he has adopted a policy of hands off in its making. Otherwise its course would have been more competently ordered and its evils eliminated. Since God is visualized in terms of totalitarian righteousness, in imitative contradistinction to the evil totalitarian political state, it is only natural that stress should fall upon divine transcendence, excessive dissimilarity to everything human, and unconditional cosmic authority. But this way of thinking nullifies man's experience of divine fellowship in the making of history. It denies the immanence of God in the moral, rational, and spiritual strivings of men who believe themselves to have been made in the image of God. It empties all reality out of the lives of prophets and saints who have thought themselves to be God's spokesmen and co-workers in shaping the destiny of the world. And it bemoans the vanity of all devout men who have spent their lives in the struggle to bring the Kingdom of God a little nearer to realization among mankind.

The modern advocates of historical dualism have rendered a useful service by vividly calling attention to the fact of evil in the world. And the specific age to which they belong has been peculiarly suited to produce this awareness. From time to time human society needs to be jolted out of a complacency to which it all too readily succumbs. Undoubtedly, the patient has become ill; but he has often been so before, and it is rather hasty to conclude that this recent indisposition is a sickness unto death. One readily concedes that nature is cruel, that man is vicious, and that society is corrupt. But he is blind indeed who cannot see that the heavens declare the glory of God, who cannot perceive that man bears the ineffaceable image of his Divine Maker, and who fails to appreciate the progress of the last twenty centuries in creating a human society that approaches a little nearer to the ideal Kingdom of God. To separate God from human history may save his theoretical righteousness, but it does so at the expense of his sustaining fatherhood, on which the religious life of mankind is nourished. Removing God from the scene of daily temporal happenings is like prescribing a deadly potion to cure a temporary illness. It is as if the surgeon were to order the excision of the throbbing heart when the patient needs only a corrective appendectomy.

Every historian knows that the conflict between

[123]

good and evil is a continuous process in the evolution of human culture. But to cut the Gordian knot by declaring the struggle hopeless in the present world and to posit a separate area of history under a divine regime in which evil has no existence is too easy and too hasty a resolution of the problem. Actual history exhibits no prospect of working itself out in that manner. Like the mills of the gods, the cycles of the centuries grind slowly but surely. Thus far they show no inclination to cease their revolutions or to relieve man of responsibility for working out his own salvation under such measure of divine guidance as is available for him in this present evil world. By arbitrarily dividing history into two separate segments—one sphere of activity directed solely by God and the other subject exclusively to man—humans are relieved of the obligation to perform God's work in the world. But the supposition that the divine purposes will ever come to realization except through the medium of human agents is an invention of desperate men who can conceive of no other way to justify their faith in the ultimate triumph of good over evil. Impatient with the tardy accomplishments of man, they are driven to discount or ignore actual history, while they speculate on the designs of God before human history began and imaginatively read his intentions with reference to its close.

This haven of refuge is not available for those who feel compelled to face historical reality as revealed in the actual course of temporal events. The beginnings of human culture fade out into the oblivion of a remote antiquity, and the end stretches away into the impenetrable regions of the distant future. But the concretely observable segment, increasing constantly with the flow of time, supplies the specific facts with which one must deal. This history has been and still is made by living men, and its quality is conditioned by the persistence of their struggle to overcome evil with good. The key to success is human activism inspired by the desire to make the world a better place in which to live. In the language of religion, this means the attempt of each successive generation to bring a little nearer to realization the Kingdom of God on earth. The process is constant and unending. When one ideal has been attained, another looms upon the horizon and challenges further effort. Each new vision is a fresh revelation of the divine will and an imperious summons to human action. From this point of view God and man must be thought of as working together in shaping the course of history as it takes form on the terrestrial plane, and one who would understand its significance must view it in its entirety as a continuous stream of actual events.

CHAPTER V

THE CONTINUITY OF HISTORY

THE world grows older day by day. The yester-days, ceaselessly following one another, form countless links in the endless chain of time. How or when this process will end, like how or when it began, are questions that yield no ready answer. The beginning and the end of individuals who participate in this constant flow of time are matters capable of definite comprehension, but the perpetuity of the process itself eludes our finite grasp. One of the greatest obstacles to an understanding of the significance of history is the difficulty of apprehending the full meaning of the fact of continuity.

A. THE COMPLEXITY OF EVENTS

The phenomena of history are highly pluralistic. Events are infinite in their variety, unlimited in their frequency, and unpredictable in their recurrence. Writers of history strive to impose coherence upon this mottled landscape by selecting a specific series of incidents to the exclusion of all others, or by plotting the territory into distinctive chronological periods, or by pursuing some hypothetical sequence of cause and effect assumed to furnish the key to an understanding of the whole. This artificial procedure helps to simplify the historian's task and lends a semblance of order to an otherwise impenetrable labyrinth of promiscuous happenings.

Political history is one of the oldest types to invite the attention of historians. The story of nations and empires, told in terms of rulers and their conquests, is a familiar form of narrative. The annals of Egyptian, Babylonian, Assyrian, and Persian princes, composed to glorify the deeds of mighty war lords, bulk large in our records of the past. Greek history often seems to be pre-eminently the account of battles fought for the possession of Troy, of conflicts between Athens and Sparta, of the heroic defense against Persian invaders, and of the political triumphs of Alexander the Great. The glory of Rome begins with Julius Caesar's conquest of Gaul and continues with the imperial regime of Augustus and his successors. The history of Europe down to the present moment is one long series of internal conflicts between rival princes and nations.

The discovery of the Western Hemisphere provided a new arena for politics and war. Spaniards, Englishmen, and Frenchmen fought for control of the new territory until the New England revolution gave birth to another autonomous nation. It, in turn, consolidated its domains by further military struggles against native Indian tribes, against continuing English and Spanish rivals, and against recalcitrant groups within its own borders. As this military type of civilization spread to Japan, China, India, and Africa, it carried in its train those ideals of political ascendancy that

[127]

transformed the history of these territories into a record of the activities of armies and navies devoted to the maintenance of national dignity. History today is still being made in terms of political events on a world scale.

Biblical history is no exception to the primacy of interest in politics. The Hebrews possessed themselves of Canaan by military force. They organized a monarchy to provide effective resistance against aggression from without. Later, in order to compensate for the failure of political institutions to insure final triumph over their foes, they phrased their ideal society in terms of a coming "Kingdom of God." Christianity carried forward the same tradition. When, after three centuries of struggle, the new religion won the support of the political authorities of the Roman Empire, it adopted as its practical role the program of the "church militant." Its God was the supreme monarch of the universe, who ultimately would so thoroughly conquer all enemies that none would ever venture again to raise a rebellious head.

In the meantime the militant church pressed forward to new victories. It assumed responsibility for maintaining political order in the governments of Europe. It evangelized the Saxons at the point of the sword. It sponsored those two centuries of holy warfare called the Crusades, in which the Western peoples vainly sought to wrest the Holy Land from its Moslem conquerors. When the expanding social life of Europe produced greater diversity within Christianity, rival branches of this religion savagely fought one another at the behest of princely protectors. The wars of religion have been among the bitterest in the annals of history.

Politics and religion still remain so closely allied in our traditional ways of thinking that Christian history is often written as though it had been merely a subsidiary phase of national life. Or religion may be made the primary concern while politics is assigned a subordinate position—not, however, to be severed from religion. One large branch of Christendom, Roman Catholicism, still maintains the rightful supremacy of church over state. Even Protestants still talk and act as though politics and religion were inseparably bound together either as synthesis or antithesis. In practically every Christian assembly one can count upon the popularity of such military hymns as "Onward, Christian Soldiers" or "The Son of God Goes Forth to War." And we still define our religious task to be the establishment of a "Kingdom" of God. It is little wonder that history has sometimes been curtly termed "past politics."

A more intensive scrutiny into the processes of history reveals a complexity of factors only remotely, if at all, connected with political happenings. The human quest for food and shelter long antedates political institutions. The latter emerged at a relatively advanced stage of social development, when techniques were devised for maintaining the integrity and prosperity of national groups or for satisfying their territorial ambitions. The historian is wont to become absorbed in the paraphernalia of governments because these matters have been most abundantly recorded, but he ought not to forget that it is the existence of the obscure or forgotten man that provides the stream of human life on whose bosom history is borne along in its devious course. Without the persistence of the commonalty of mankind there would be no real human history of any sort. In that event neither politics nor religion nor any other feature of our so-called "civilization" could have arisen or survived.

Ultimately the historical quest aims to recover the total story of the career of mankind on the surface of the earth. Generation after generation of men is born, lives, and dies in a never ending stream of time. They participate in a wide variety of commonplace activities. Physical environments condition their manner of living. They adjust themselves as best they can to temperature, climate, and terrain. When they have so mastered their environment that they can eat, sleep, and pass their waking hours in safety, they undertake new conquests, inspired by curiosity, imagination, and desire. They order their living according to habituated schedules; they give rein more or less freely to their passions; they pass judgments of value upon activities and attainments; they devise amusements for their leisure time; they explore new areas of intellectual interest; they indulge their appetites for art and music and literature; they formulate moral codes to control hatred and cupidity and lust; they rear institutions to conserve past attainments and insure an orderly group life; they practice religious rites and define proper beliefs—in short, they build a civilization.

The structure of civilization has been slow in building, and its full culmination may even yet be a long way off. It is still a going and a growing concern. Its beginnings reach back into the shadowy past from which no records have survived. Sometimes we compromise with our ignorance by calling these times a "prehistoric age," but it is quite erroneous to assume that the people who lived then have no importance for the genesis and evolution of our cultural heritage. They are still the hidden foundation on which much of the superstructure rests. It is from them that mankind has inherited its appetites, its passions, its physical energies, its powers of imagination, its unconquerable urge toward the mastery of environments, its tardy capacity for moral development, and its belated yearnings for spiritual conquests. These elemental impulses, tutored by centuries of accumulating experience, are still the raw materials that have to be built into the texture of human civilization.

Many different patterns and a wide variety of accomplishments were the inevitable result of this slowly moving process of growth. The more intensively the historian seeks unity and coherence in rehearsing the story of the past, the greater may be his bafflement over the evident fact of limitless complexity. Perhaps the best that he can do is to plot those crisscross highways that come within the range of his restricted vision. Indeed, it may be that the world is still too young to have produced, as yet, any single trunk line for routing civilization's traffic from the dawn of creation to its consummation in eternity. Naturally the historian desires comprehensive and perfect knowledge, but unfortunately he is dealing with a subject that refuses to yield itself in its entirety to temporal and spatial limitations.

The rise and decline of specific cultures tempt one to philosophize about history. By arbitrarily restricting attention to selected segments of the past the historian ventures to discover the inner character of the total process and to predict its ultimate outcome. He passes lightly over distracting variations, ignores many of the tributaries that have contributed to the volume of the ambling stream, and postulates some theory to explain the origin and end of world events. Thus he fits the entire course of civilization into a single hypothetical pattern. As Oswald Spengler would have us believe, the hourglass of time is about to run out with no power at hand to reverse the instrument. Blind fate is the heartless mistress who leads man to a mountain top of attainment only to plunge him, willing or unwilling, headlong into the eternal valley of despair. At the opposite pole the millennial prophet, no less pessimistic in his evaluation of past events, forecasts a glorious triumph; presently God himself will destroy this evil world and institute a new order of existence upon a miraculously renovated earth.

[132]

Prognostications of this sort are merely desperate and futile attempts to evade the stern facts of historical complexity and unending continuity. Alleged collapses of civilization are only transitory stages in the emergence of some new series of events that compel us to reshuffle our old standards of value and strive with fresh ardor for the attainment of further ends that may be esteemed desirable. It is folly to grow impatient over the leisurely processes of time, as though its storehouse of centuries were about to become exhausted. One need have no fear that there will not be ample days ahead for new experiences and experiments in the making of history. It might well be said of ages, as of individuals, that they rise on stepping-stones of their dead selves to higher things. In order to understand the past, we must recognize that history is constantly on the move. It is a continuous product of human living by a great multitude of different persons in widely varied settings and under the impulsion of diverse interests. One must not lose sight of the infinite variety and perpetual continuity that inhere in the historical course of events.

B. THE MODERN PAST AND THE ANCIENT PRESENT

The continuity of the present with the past is not always duly appreciated. It has often been said that a modern student habitually reconstructs history in accordance with some dominating present-day interest. Must we not admit that the very urge to find meaning in the events of bygone days prompts one to assign to those happenings a significance which they did not originally possess? Consequently, strict historical objectivity is declared to be impossible of attainment; the would-be historian inevitably distorts his picture of the past. These historical "relativists," as they are called, maintain that the present indelibly stamps its own image upon any attempted reading of earlier events. Otherwise it is thought that one would have no lively concern with the career of his ancestors.

It may be very true that lack of objectivity has been one of the historian's besetting sins. But it is equally hazardous to try to understand the processes of life today without comprehending the essential continuity of the historical stream. It is a mere truism to say that, over wide ranges of human impulses, actions, and thinking, the past was remarkably modern. Apart from the strong tendency which men have always felt to imitate their ancestors, the unity of history has been insured by the very perpetuity of the human organism that acts in the making of history, as well as by the permanence of the physical setting in which life itself is maintained. Not only does one inherit from his forebears the mechanism that conditions the emotional, mental, and spiritual urges of life, but the social and cultural environments from which the take-off for creative living is made are, in large measure, a holdover from antiquity.

The modern man's pride in the advanced status of his civilization may be due for a shock when he becomes better acquainted with some of his remote ancestors. Then he discovers that they pursued the same quests that entice him, that they employed similar means for the realization of their desires, and that their efforts were crowned with a like mixture of failure and success. They strove, as do we, by methods of trial and error, to build permanent institutions of government for tribes, races, nations, or empires. They endeavored to make their armies and navies invincible by means of the best available equipment. The Greek phalanx and the Roman trireme were inspired by the same motives that have engendered modern *Panzer* units and superdreadnoughts. The deification of physical force still perpetuates the same human passions that prompted the caveman to wield a heavier club than any of his rivals could command. In this respect the ancients were thoroughly, though less efficiently, modern.

Over a wide range of experience and action past generations have pursued careers and faced problems that anticipated events and opinions familiar in the life of today. Two thousand years ago Cicero, anxious about his wayward son, who was about to be expelled from the University of Athens while the father at home had a divorce suit on his hands, might have been a twentieth-century man. In quite modern fashion Nero built himself a house equipped with a hot-air heating plant and an elaborate system of up-to-date plumbing. Cicero and Plutarch justified in thoroughly modern style the military conquests of Alexander the Great and the triumphs of the Roman armies. Plutarch said that barbarian peoples had been vanquished by Alexander for their own good, since otherwise they would have missed the real blessings of a superimposed civilization. Left to themselves, they never would have learned to read Homer and sing the tragedies of Euripides and Sophocles! Cicero conceded that war was a brutish business to be undertaken only by a just and wise state like Rome, which had in view the elimination of all wars by forcing its beneficent will upon the whole earth. Seneca sounds almost ultra-modern when he protests against the folly and wastefulness of all forms of military strife and bemoans the plain insanity of men rushing in anger against their fellows whom they have never seen and disrupting with their navies the quiet of the seas that God had created for the peaceful transportation of the world's traffic.

Today's industrial and commercial developments far exceed anything accomplished by the ancients, but the ambition and avarice that so frequently attend these activities were well known to antiquity. In this respect the past was genuinely modern. The imperial conquerors of ancient times were chiefly motivated by insatiable greed for taxes and plunder from subjugated peoples. The rich manifested no scruples of conscience in selling the poor for silver and the needy for a pair of shoes. Profiteering from the misfortune or necessity of others was a very ancient human weakness that still survives, however much the modern wolf may garb himself in the skin of the innocent sheep. The underlying human impulse to drive a sharp bargain, to enslave the weak for the advantage of the strong, to covet the goods of one's neighbor, and to amass for one's self, by fair means or foul, a superabundance of earthly possessions, is no recent or modern ingredient in the human makeup.

The ancients knew, as well as do we, that the love of money is the root of much evil. Among those who had committed crimes against the welfare of humanity, Pliny the Elder listed, first, the man who had introduced the use of gold rings and, second, the one who first coined the gold denarius. Thereafter avarice and the love of display cast their baneful shadow over human history. Pseudo-Sallust in a letter to the emperor (probably Trajan) advised him that the greatest service he could confer on his country was to extirpate, or at least diminish, the excessive love of money. Livy lamented that the poverty and frugality once held in high honor among the Romans had given way to a degrading passion for wealth and excessive pleasures. Both moralists and historians dwelt much upon this theme and railed against the corrupting influence of luxury. As the poor grew more impecunious, the well-to-do indulged in lavish expenditures. They provided themselves with elaborate country seats; their premises were overrun with hordes of domestics; they adorned their houses with gold and silver decorations and costly works of art; both men and women practiced extravagant ornamentation in dress; they wasted their substance on elaborate banquets and expensive shows; and they squandered large sums of money on precious stones purchased from foreign or hostile merchants. This catalogue of vices which the ancient critic charged against his contemporaries sounds very like a modern arraignment of the rich by some of our zealous social reformers.

Even the amenities of civilization cultivated by moderns were not totally strange to the ancients. They reached a remarkable degree of attainment in various spheres of artistic, intellectual, and spiritual activity. The urge toward self-expression and communion with one another resulted in the development of some of the finest examples of language and literature. When men today feel a need to enlarge the vocabulary of current speech, they still revert to the Greek or Latin tongues for words or phrases to express their meaning. Classical standards continue to be models for good literary style. In the realms of pictorial art, sculpture, architecture, and music the products of the past continue to enrich our modern culture. We readily recognize that the ancients were quite as keenly attuned as are we to the higher realms of cultural life in linguistic, literary, and artistic accomplishments. In these spheres their modernity is beyond question.

Again, in the field of intellectual effort called "philosophy" the ancients are often our contemporaries. They possessed the same qualities of inquisitive mentality as do moderns. They felt the same urge to peer behind the veil that hangs between the world of sense-perception and the far-flung invisibilities of cosmic space. They were not equipped with our mechanical

devices of microscope, telescope, and physical labora-
tories that have pushed the curtain a little farther back
upon the stage, but on the more distant horizon we
still find them as competent as are we to speculate
about the secrets of the hidden universe. Their natural
powers of observation, their adherence to logical con-
sistency, their quest for truth and beauty and goodness, and their efforts to enthrone virtue above vice
make them thoroughly at home in a company of modern philosophers. And there is a distinct aura of modernity about Origen, the noted Christian philosopher
of the third century, who pursued a literary career
with the aid of a bevy of secretaries and an aggressive
publisher to sponsor the circulation of his scholarly
productions.

In the religious sphere the continuity between past
and present is especially pronounced. According to ordinary modes of thinking, the ancients anticipated the
total range of modern needs in the area of religious
interests and activities. One commonly assumes that
his forefathers devised the type of religious institution
that can best serve the present-day demand. Also, they
are thought to have formulated the content of doctrine valid for all time to come, to have prescribed
rules for conduct on all future occasions, and to have
exhibited ideal examples of attainment in personal
piety. Whether or not these assumptions are strictly
true does not alter the evident fact of strong historical
continuity in the religious features of our evolving
civilization.

If the past is modern, it is equally true that the present is ancient. That fact is only the reverse side of the same coin. In hundreds of ways life today is a replica of the past. A wide range of habitual procedures in thought and action perpetuate themselves without any consciousness of their historical genesis in antiquity. The very cut of the garments we wear conserves the tradition of the ancients. Men still insist on having buttons sewed to the sleeves of their coats, despite the fact that they have long ago abandoned the custom of attaching the cuffs which the buttons were originally designed to hold in place. Present-day civilization is still burdened or blessed with a great mass of traditional holdovers from bygone ages.

In large areas of cultural life the tendency to preserve the customs of the ancients is still apparent. We maintain that ideals in government shall perpetuate the principles laid down by George Washington and conform to the notions of the authors of the Bill of Rights or of the framers of the American Constitution. The political pronouncements of antiquity are thought to constitute permanent rules for the guidance of opinion and conduct. Our religionists are similarly concerned to justify their beliefs and practices by reference to the normative past. In literature, art, and music the imitation of ancient models remains the standard for testing excellence. The traditions of industry, trade, and commerce emulate the customs of the past. Education is often assumed to be the acquisition of knowledge and techniques developed by the forefathers. In every sphere of life, being the children that we are, we seek to conserve the heritage that has been bequeathed to us by our older predecessors. The past flows into the present in the continuous stream of life.

C. THE NEW WORLD OF TODAY

Notwithstanding our reverence for the past, life in the present age is beset by many novelties. It offers a welter of experiences and problems that have never before been confronted by mankind. If a cross-section of civilization as it existed barely two hundred years ago is placed beside a similar segment from modern times, the contrast becomes immediately apparent. The mechanization of the processes of life, so pervasive today, was then utterly unknown. Railroads and steamships were as yet undreamed of. Electricity smote men with the deadly lightning, but no steps had been taken to harness it to their machines, to make it light their dwellings, or to convert it into power to carry their messages by wire and air throughout the world. Those were the benighted horse-and-buggy days, when men knew nothing of modern facilities in transportation by automobile, airplane, and stream-lined Diesel-driven speedsters of the rails.

Industrial conditions have been radically transformed even in a single century. Machines have been exalted, and human individuality abased. The scattered workshops of single artisans have been displaced by the central factory with its steam or electrically driven equipment. The personality of the workman loses itself in the totality of the human mass that daily streams in and out of the factory's doors. Group life develops a distinctive consciousness and creates an entirely new set of social problems for ethical and religious thinking. At the same time, manufacturers and capitalists combine to control production and markets and to protect their interests against the aggressions of united labor. Business conditions create a new type of life to which the simpler codes of personal living seem inadequate or inapplicable. Modern industrial and commercial activity is an affair of the new world the like of which was totally unknown to the ancients.

The last century's acquisitions in knowledge have created virtually a new heaven and a new earth. In grandfather's Bible there was a note on the margin at the head of the first chapter of the Book of Genesis placing the date of the world's creation in the year 4004 B.C. A hundred years ago the approximate accuracy of this date was generally accepted. In the meantime the science of geology has constructed a totally new account of terrestrial history, reaching back through millenniums of time. The origins of man and the beginnings of social life take their start in a far distant past, out of which order and cultural achievements have only slowly and gradually emerged. Man's original kinship is with the beasts, whose blood still flows in his veins. The task of making goodness prevail is no longer a mere question of eliminating the consequences of Adam's sin and restoring a perfection thus temporarily lost. It is the much more difficult

[142]

problem of infusing into human life new moral and spiritual ideals and aspirations to overcome effectively the original bestial heritage.

The growth of historical knowledge has undermined much of our former faith in the ideal character of the past. As the ancients have become better known, their shortcomings have become more conspicuous. The "debunkers" of history are not always pleasant companions, and they are quite as prone to exaggerate the evils of the past as our authoritarian idealists are inclined to magnify its virtues. But the truth is that evil and good have always been inextricably mixed in the history of mankind and that the supposed existence of a once golden age, when the world was free from misfortune and distress, is either the pure creation of a poetic imagination or a partial reading of history by which one selects and amplifies the tolerably good but ignores the reprehensible evils. Life in the modern world constantly streams out of the yesterdays, carrying forward in its current numerous particles of both good and evil; but it flows continually forward, to be enlarged by new tributaries and colored by the new terrain through which it takes its course. While it is partially a replica of the past, it is also a distinctly new thing under the sun.

Contemporary living is thus always a new enterprise. Not only does the individual travel a road that he has never before explored, but it is also a highway that none of his predecessors has been able to plot with certainty. He must negotiate hazardous turns that are marked on no maps. On his own responsibility he must choose his course at forks in the road where signboards are lacking. He must traverse steep grades and sharp declines that suddenly spring out of the unknown. If he finds himself on the wrong road, he must retrace his course and experiment with another route. He must be prepared for unmarked dips in the pavement, sudden blockades of traffic, unaccountable perversities of other drivers, and all the various menaces to safety that stalk on the highway of life.

The educational value of acquaintance with the past is, of course, highly important. It would be sheer folly to repeat ways of living that have been proved unfruitful, and the imitation of good models is always an excellent discipline. But to plan one's course in the world of today as though it could be a literal copy of what has been done in the past, or to assume that antiquity can furnish patterns for every form of present-day thinking and conduct, will lead one into a double fallacy. It will result in failure to appreciate the significance of modern times as a new age packed with facts and issues that were entirely unknown to the ancients. They cannot be required to have made pronouncements upon, or to have provided solutions for, questions of whose existence they had not the slightest inkling. And, in the second place, when moderns strive only to imitate the past, they relinquish by this very attitude their birthright to constructive and aggressive leadership in the solution of today's most important problems.

Perhaps the lag so widely felt in the cultural development of modern times is largely due to the still prevalent custom of aping the past instead of venturing boldly upon new paths of exploration in the present. Old prescriptions are followed for the treatment of new diseases; and, when they fail, the maladies are pronounced incurable. Venturesome persons who would blaze a new trail are commonly viewed with suspicion or persecuted for heresy. A peculiar sanctity attaches to the intrenched privileges of tradition; the ways of the fathers are sacred in their own right. And so a benumbing lethargy afflicts men when they come face to face with the problem of discarding old procedures and devising new techniques for the treatment of current issues. The rank and file of humanity do not want to be the first by whom the new is tried, and they are often quite content to be counted among the last by whom the old is set aside. One imagines that there is a static stability about civilization that makes it more secure when standing still than when moving onward from the dead past through the living present into the unknown future.

Aggressive living in the immediate present is always something of a venture. Driven by fresh urges toward thought and action, one may envisage a happy outcome but must at the same time be prepared for disappointments. If we fear defeat more than we love healthful endeavor, it will be unwise for us to explore new highways. But if reverses, accepted with stoic fortitude and used as tutors in experience, become new

[145]

incentives to further action, the challenge and zest of living will yield their own rewards. And the hope of making some constructive contribution toward the betterment of the contemporary world will relieve that sense of futility and aimlessness that may otherwise settle down like a deadly blight upon aspiring souls.

Opportunities for venturesome living rise before us on every hand in the modern world. All of our customs and institutions tend to grow stale with age and call for the services of individuals capable of reforming, revitalizing, or supplementing the heritages handed down from the past. If the world has been growing worse, it is because mankind has not arisen to meet this challenge; and, if it is growing better, that improved status is due to persistent and repeated human endeavor. Civilization as a product of man's activity refuses to stand still, and the price of progress has to be paid in the coinage of strenuous human living. Political ills will never be removed by blind and unthinking allegiance to a party machine. Help can come only from voters willing to think, criticize, and act for the correction of current abuses. Social evils will never be remedied except as men give themselves to the arduous task of analyzing causes and devising new modes of procedure in dealing with the discoverable facts. To preach the application of some rule of thumb lifted ready-made out of the past can at best be only a temporary palliative but never a permanent cure. Moral disorders can never be abolished simply by prophetic denunciations or even by legislative restraints. Valuable as these means are, they will fail of their purpose unless substantially supplemented by an understanding of genetic conditions and a persistent education in the making of virtue. Even religion is subject to decadence except as its representatives so live that they become mediums for new truth and light to break through upon the temporal scene.

Each generation is the creator of its own changing culture. The world of today will be good or bad in proportion to the creative energy displayed by man throughout the vast areas of activity over which he exercises control. If we think to live in comfortable enjoyment of the deposits of virtue bequeathed to us by the ancients, we are courting disappointment. A new age demands the cultivation of new virtues that must well up out of life today. Admiration for the attainments of our ancestors is the springboard from which we make our take-off into modern life, but fresh achievements will be the constructive work of our own hands. We look to the past for instruction and inspiration while we attempt new accomplishments in the present.

Indeed, it has been truly said that it is we who are the ancients. The age of the world has been increasing throughout all past centuries, and today we are the children of its greatest antiquity. Our ancestors belonged to a more youthful generation, while we are the products of its greater maturity. We stand on the shoulders of all those who have come before us; their experience and wisdom are in our possession, and it is our privilege to be wiser and more efficient than they have been. As knowledge grows from more to more, and reverence for the mystery of life increases, the immaturity of primitive times gives way to a riper wisdom and a larger capacity for building more perfectly the superstructure of civilization. It is the duty of modern men to add to the achievements of the ancients, to make themselves not only the equals but the superiors of their ancestors, and to become the exponents of truer insights and more competent performance in the business of living. Thus history, which is in constant motion, may be marked by progressive development.

D. THE QUEST FOR MEANING

One who has become keenly awake to the fact of historical continuity may still be puzzled about the meaning that attaches to this process. If he seeks to understand it in terms of something external to itself, he will postulate some stable first cause, like the unmoved mover of Aristotelian speculation, to account for the variety of historical events and reduce them to some uniform system of interpretation. This single hypothetical force may be only a blind fate, or it may be the regulative power of natural law, or it may be Hegel's absolute spirit continually striving to come to self-expression, or it may be an all-controlling economic urge, or it may be the activity of a transcendental Deity, or the machinations of a perverse Satan, or whatever else seems most satisfactorily to provide a concept of stability to impose upon the distracting picture of promiscuous events in the perpetual flux of time.

On the other hand, one who looks for meaning strictly within the process itself has a more difficult task. His primary interest will be to discover ways and means by which the process may be kept going in useful directions and without loss of momentum. He is not concerned to find outside of history something that is totally unhistorical to account for the significance of specific events. Rather, he strives to read meaning out of temporal occurrences, instead of stretching them upon the Procrustean bed of some extra-temporal hypothesis. If he formulates historical laws, they must never transcend the bounds of experimental knowledge; and, since history is continually in the making, its supposed laws will always be subject to revision in the light of further observation. If God is found in history, he will be the Deity whose self-revelation is being continually enlarged as the human observer grows in apperceptive sensitivity. This God is himself a participant in the eternal flow of historical evolution.

To give history meaning by deducing from it practical instruction for the guidance of contemporary life is a very ancient custom. This is a familiar note throughout the Bible, and it is sounded repeatedly by Greek and Roman historians. But on this procedure values were found less in the historical process as a whole than in outstanding atomistic events, which in the case of the biblical writers were special acts of divine intervention in mundane affairs. The Greeks and Romans fixed their gaze more specifically upon human activity, from which they sought to derive valuable lessons. Thucydides thought history useful as a means of making men familiar with the type of occurrence that is pretty sure to happen again, and thus they may learn beforehand how it should be met. Polybius was especially insistent upon the instructive value of past events to guide the decisions of statesmen in times of both peace and war. Diodorus and Plutarch added a moral emphasis; men who knew the past would become aware of the good to be imitated and the evil to be shunned. It was naïvely assumed that anyone who had acquired this knowledge would wish to pursue virtue and avoid vice. Similarly, the Roman Cicero lauded history as "the witness of the ages, the light of truth and the mistress of life." Livy composed his monumental *History of Rome* in order that future generations might know what to imitate and what to shun. And Tacitus designed his annals to serve as a guide to virtue by warning men from a course of action that might bring down upon them the censures of posterity; history was a deterrent from depravity in word and deed.

When attention is centered upon the continuity of the historical stream, instead of upon individual happenings, the quest for meaning reaches beyond those pragmatic values that may quite properly inhere in specific persons or events and strives to comprehend the nature and significance of the process as a whole. What are the factors within the stream itself that keep it in motion, and how firm can one's faith be in its future?

Faith in the future of history has often been challenged. The subject has elicited a vast amount of pessimism. Frequently the biblical writers were so overcome by the evils of the present age that they could see no hope except in its complete dissolution to make way for a totally new age to be miraculously introduced by God himself. Even the more hopeful persons among the Greeks and the Romans could not entertain the notion of a continuous historical development. They were able to conceive only of cycles of advancement and degeneration following one another in endless rotation. Culture was like a ship tossed on a turbulent ocean. It might rise on the crest of one wave today, but tomorrow it would descend again to the trough of the sea, continuing its ups and downs without cessation.

Current evils, magnified by their proximity, have often occasioned much discouragement about the future. When one imagines that of late things have been going from bad to worse, this psychology begets grave doubts about the character of coming events. Civilization is said to have become fatally diseased or to have suffered shipwreck. In desperation we may propose some stimulus to restore activity to its enfeebled frame, or we may attempt to salvage as much as possible from the wreckage. But, at best, it is believed to be a bird with a broken pinion who will never again soar to those heights where formerly it sported in full strength.

Pessimism about the future is a very old and frequently recurring state of mind. Cicero believed that the Roman government was destined to endure forever, because, if it failed, the catastrophe could be likened only to the final wreck of the universe. Yet Rome fell and civilization sprang up with new vigor from its ruins. When the Gothic hordes under Alaric sacked Rome, it seemed to Jerome from his monastic sanctuary in Bethlehem that the eye of the world had been put out. She who had been the mother of nations had become their tomb. Jerome was unable to envisage the new nations that were to arise from the grave of his "eternal" city. Two centuries later Gregory the Great, blinded by the devastations wrought by the Lombards in Italy, thought that even the church was like a leaky ship whose rotting timbers must soon disintegrate as the end of the present world drew near. Nevertheless, the church survived and prospered even in Italy for many centuries after the time of Gregory.

In the fourteenth century, following the scourge of the Black Death that is believed to have swept away from one-third to one-half the population of Europe, a heavy atmosphere of despair settled down upon society. But presently the processes of recovery once more demonstrated their irrepressible vitality. At the opening of the nineteenth century the Napoleonic wars

births of cultural development. It is in this mysterious fact that one seeks the ultimate meaning of history.

Is history just a fortuitous concourse of atomistic events, as an Epicurean might say, or is it a product of innate forces whose secrets may be hard to discover but whose driving force cannot be ignored with impunity? At least two distinct types of influence must be recognized in the making of history: it is a product of material existences belonging to a widely varied physical world, and it is also made by human beings who are something more than mere physical entities. They possess, in lower or higher degree, emotional and imaginative faculties, a mind capable of learning by experience, ability to entertain desires and form judgments, a disposition to estimate values, powers of choice between possible alternatives, and wills to pursue specific courses of action. This means that history has both a material and a spiritual content. But these elements are so intricately entwined and confusingly blended as to render very difficult any attempt to decipher the inner significance of the total process.

If history is pictured merely on the analogy of physical nature, one may easily become resigned to the seeming inevitability of its procedures. The human body is something given man by birth; the air he breathes and the food he eats are supplied by an environment over which he has little or no control; the length of his days on earth is normally not a matter of his own choosing; and his powers of body and mind are limited by conditions over which he has only very restricted dominion. One might infer from these facts that man's responsibility for the making of history reduces itself to a virtual zero; he merely does what physical conditions foreordain. Since an oak always produces an oak, it would be nonsense to say to the acorn: "Now grow yourself into a sprig of heather or a flowering hyacinth." Nor does the acorn need to fear that it will become only a thistle. So it might be thought absurd to expect men to produce any sort of history different from that which they have made in the past.

This is only one element in the picture; nor is it by any means the most significant one. While man is a natural animal, he is also possessed of spiritual capacities; he has powers of thought and choice and decision that the oak has never acquired. He inherits nature, but nurture also comes within the range of his grasp. He can, if he so wills, seal the acorn in a block of cement and thus completely thwart its power to grow, or he can nourish it in a fertile soil and by his skilful manipulation produce from it an oak mightier than any of its predecessors. He may even graft upon its stem cuttings from other trees that will, in the end, yield a result such as has never previously been seen. Thus, by means of nurture he can transcend or transform nature. It is this spiritual freedom of man—his pursuit of choices, the exercise of his will, the determinative effect of his decisions, his susceptibility to ideals, his response to envisaged values, his feeling of communion with unseen forces, his yearning for larger knowledge, his restless quest for new experiences—that constitutes his chief significance for the making of human history.

The continuity of history exhibits a perpetual fusion of material facts and spiritual activities. In general it may be said that the former are stable and the latter variable. Gold and marble and common soil are historically indifferent until man brings to bear upon them his skill and his will. One can readily believe that men have been more inclined to exercise their initiative upon the physical materials at their disposal than upon improving the quality of their spiritual selves. Their technology tends to outrun their moral and religious attainments. But the relation of these material and spiritual interests to one another as they have been operating since the dawn of time and the importance of this knowledge for present and future generations give history its ultimate significance. This we may call the "religious meaning" of the past.

CHAPTER VI

THE RELIGIOUS SIGNIFICANCE OF HISTORY

THE past has long enjoyed unique distinction as a teacher of the present. Especially in the sphere of religion has the voice of antiquity been the voice of authority. Every well-established cult has, from time immemorial, justified its procedures by reference to history. Its officials are believed to hold their position by right of tradition; its ceremonies derive their validity from ancestral practice; and its teachings embody the supposedly superior wisdom of primitive times. Each new generation of adherents strives faithfully to reproduce the rites, the beliefs, and the ideals of its ancestors. And the customs of the ancients, when rehearsed by bards, priests, legislators, and sages, become inexorable laws of the gods.

Christians have been particularly diligent in attaching religious significance to the past. They took over from Judaism reverence for the ancient scriptures and soon added a group of canonized books from early Christian times. Tradition was enthroned on the seat of authority. It became the distinctive task of the Christian leader to perpetuate the sacred heritage received from his predecessors. The truth to be taught, the practices to be followed, and the ideals to be pursued were to be modeled after patterns authoritatively decreed in earlier days. The past yielded infallible norms for life in the present and the future.

A. THE THEORY OF A NORMATIVE PAST

The custom of making the past the authoritative teacher of the present rests upon an interpretation of history that has long prevailed in Christian thinking. History has been viewed as a series of successive ages, with each displaying distinctive characteristics assumed to inhere in its very nature. According to the Jewish notion, all the events of the past had taken place in conformity with a prearranged plan of God. He had assigned to each age its distinctive quality and would continue to do so for all future time. Similarly, Christians adopted the segmental scheme of history and treated specific eras as though they might have existed independently of one another in watertight compartments of space.

The segmental arrangement of history tends to idealize the earlier and less well-known periods. If it is true that the evil done by men lives after them while "the good is oft interred with their bones," just the opposite course has been the fact with reference to those impersonal blocks of time called "ages." The more remote the period, the more highly has it been revered, and the more surely have its defects been buried in the ashes of forgetfulness. In comparison with the present the past seems to be the golden age, and the more remote it is the more aureous is its halo.

The normal counterpart of an idealized past is the theory of a decadent present. The course of history is thought to have moved steadily in the descending scale. As the Greeks had said, the golden age lay in the gray dawn of antiquity, and by a gradual process of decay the final age of iron had at last enveloped mortals. A similar idea prevailed among both Jews and Christians. The world had been at its best the day it came fresh from the hand of the Creator, but almost immediately it began to deteriorate. Yet it had not been left to grow old unrelieved. From time to time, by the mouth of legislator, prophet, or wise man, God had vouchsafed remedial messages of instruction. Thus the past came to have a double authority. Not only did it carry one back to the early days when mankind was at its best in an Eden-like perfection; it also gave one access to historical moments when fresh utterances of Deity had been explicitly recorded in the pages of scripture.

For one who still holds to this time-honored view of history the religious significance of the past is no problem. Its primary meaning lies in its normative significance. It is the one authoritative guide in all matters of religion. Doctrine, procedure, organization—all are to be authenticated by reference to antiquity. But modern scientific methods of inquiry introduced into the field of history have slowly undermined the foundations on which the dogma of an ideally normative past had long rested secure. As educated persons adopted the evolutionary view of the world, of nature, and of man, they were forced to rethink their notions about the meaning of history for religion.

In the first place, the alleged ideality of the past suffered a severe shock at the hands of careful research into the origins of civilization. The youth of the world was found to have been a state of childlike beginnings rather than an age of slightly tarnished perfection only a short step removed from its supposed divine prototype. There was also a tremendous elongation of the time in which the course of history had been in the process of becoming. So long as one could believe that the creation of man had taken place on Friday, October 25, 4004 B.C., as Bishop Ussher had figured it out in the middle of the seventeenth century, the past was not so massive as to be beyond the possibility of easy comprehension. But when modern knowledge affirms, without a tremor of doubt, that human history began a quarter of a million years or so ago, the past becomes so unwieldy that it gets out of hand. Even the most unrestrained theorist would hardly venture nowadays to ascribe the character of ideality to those remote beginnings of the human career. The golden age of antiquity, once supposed to have been a period of paradisiac perfection for man, now evaporates in a mist of mythical fancy.

The doctrine of human decadence is not so easily surrendered. Doubtless it is a healthful sign that every age should be dissatisfied with its own attainments. And, even if we must think of history in terms of process, it does not necessarily follow that the process always moves in the direction of betterment. It would be foolhardy to assert dogmatically that men and times can never grow worse. Most of us have had experiences that testify emphatically to the contrary. But it is quite another matter to infer that the shortcomings of moderns are more abundant or reprehensible than were those of the ancients or to suppose that the present defects of society could be remedied offhand by reverting to a former status of civilization. When, discarding the theory of ideality, the historian brings out into the clear light of day every available aspect of the past, he finds that it, too, had its seamy side and that, taken in the large, a comparison of past and present yields a favorable judgment for the latter.

Modern investigation of the Jewish and Christian doctrine of revelation casts further doubt upon the authority of the past. When no questions were asked about the way in which the Bible came into existence, the book could be accepted as a direct communication from heaven. But when careful study recovered in detail the concrete circumstances under which the different parts of the biblical record arose, and when one followed through the historical process by which these writings were preserved and collected into a sacred canon, then the traditional theory of their mechanical inspiration vanished.

Thus it becomes apparent that the religious meaning of history has been greatly reduced—if it has not, in fact, been completely dissipated—so far as its supposed normative character is concerned. Perhaps it is not un-

natural that on surrendering the theory of normativeness one should abandon all thought of finding religious significance in history. The loss of a long-cher-
ished value might easily seem to mean the loss of all
values. Indeed, this change of attitude may be hailed
as a great deliverance. There may be a sense of relief in
being able to allow the dead past to bury its dead
while the living present goes about the task of working out its own salvation in terms of modern necessi-
ties and tastes.

It will soon be discovered, however, that one cannot
shuffle off the mortal coil of yesterday with so little
ceremony. In reality the yesterdays are far more enduring than we might be wont to think. Past and
present are only artificial expressions used to denote
different stages of one continuous process of time that
cannot be divided into sharply separated periods. One
generation may forget, or fail to identify, the heritage
it has derived from its ancestors, but in actual fact
there is no aspect of our modern civilization in which
the present is not deeply and widely rooted in the past.
As we have already remarked, the present is ancient
and the past is modern to a degree that is not always
fully realized. Of religion this fact is eminently true.

It would be futile to assume that so ancient an institution as the Christian church and a movement so substantially grounded in history as the Christian religion could proceed on their way at a later time with
little or no reference to their antecedents. In the often
heroic struggle to liberate ourselves from bondage to

ancient laws or customs we may have felt a desire to make a complete break with history, but in more sober moments we realize that our chief problem is not to get rid of our past. Nature at the outset has foredoomed to failure any such fanciful aspiration. We cannot cut ourselves adrift from the world that has made us what we are, but we can discard outworn formulas for estimating its meaning. We need some new and more adequate statement of history's worth for the understanding of religion.

Surrender of the normative hypothesis leaves history still an inescapable fact. It cannot be ignored by one who would refrain from playing fast and loose with reality. Even though the past is no longer in a position to command or regulate present thought and action, it still retains its instructive and stimulating value. Just because its significance is didactic rather than normative need not lessen, but may indeed increase, its worth for later times. What does actual human history teach us about religion on the terrestrial level of existence?

B. HISTORY IN THE MAKING OF RELIGION

Every enduring religion is firmly grounded in the past. This fact is particularly true of the Hebrew-Christian tradition, in which religion is intimately related to the total process of living. To be religious means to pursue a typical course of thought and action in all the relationships of life. As successive centuries have altered the texture of the contemporary culture, religious living has adjusted itself to the realities of each new era. Otherwise it would have become an irrelevant, decadent, and vanishing phenomenon. Vital religion must root itself deeply in the soil of evolving history and bear its flower and fruit in varying climates resulting from temporal and geographical expansion.

One must also remember that no historical religion ever emerged full-grown at the start. Only gradually did it acquire those features that later constituted its differentiating characteristics. Under the impact of circumstances subsequent generations of men lived and acted in the interests of certain values that seemed to them most worth while, and in this way they perpetuated and re-created that area of interest commonly termed "religion." While its institutions, its liturgies, its doctrines, its prescriptions for conduct, and the type of personal experience it nourished embraced heritages from the past, all of these legacies had to be infused with new life in the experience of each new age. One of the most elemental lessons to be learned from history is the fact that religion is integral to the process of life itself. In this sense history may be said to make religion.

The story of how historical events have determined the course of religious developments is capable of almost limitless illustration. A glance at the present religious complexion of the United States of America might puzzle a superficial observer. Its outstanding characteristic seems to be infinite complexity. Of the

Christian religion alone, there are said to be over two hundred different varieties, each branch claiming for itself exclusive genuineness. At least, membership in each of the distinctive groups gives to its adherents the largest measure of satisfaction. The historian understands how this situation has come about in the light of the development peculiar to civilization in the United States. Our shifting frontiers, our sectional autonomy, and our democratic individualism left every man free to shape his faith according to his taste. Thus our cultural history has indelibly impressed its stamp upon our religion.

Ancient times reveal the same process. The biblical records bear witness to the constant reshaping of Hebrew religion under the impact of changing events. The period of desert wanderings, the struggle for settlement in Canaan, the ultimate attainment of nationhood, and the long and tragic conflict with foreign invaders gave to Judaism a distinctive character. Lawgivers, prophets, sages, and priests had their respective tasks set for them by the conditions under which they lived. They often displayed marked originality and great creative energy in the discharge of their responsibilities, but contemporary history determined the mold into which their efforts were poured and fixed the contours of the final product.

When Christianity is approached from the historical point of view, there is the same evidence of changes wrought by the passage of time. The Christian religion survived because it was espoused by actual people who furnished the movement its living personnel. Its membership was fluid, like the processes of history. The cycle of life and death involved a constant change of adherents, and the rapid spread of the new faith about the Mediterranean world among different strata of the population quickly multiplied the diversity of its cultural contacts. Variations were an entirely normal development for a religion thus closely integrated with the historical processes of actual living. It is not surprising that there should have been different and even competing branches of Christianity before the missionary enterprise had been in vogue for even a single century.

Just because the Christian movement kept so closely in touch with real life over so wide a range of contacts did it display so many variations. There were the Pauline, the Petrine, and the Johannine branches by the close of the first century. The second century produced the Gnostic Christian teachers, who enjoyed much popularity in certain quarters. When in the next century Greek philosophy streamed into Christian thinking, an intellectual trend emerged that ultimately produced two bitter rivals—Arianism and Athanasianism. There were also Montanists, Donatists, Nestorians, and still other distinctive groups produced by the expansion of the Christian movement as it conformed to one or another interest prevalent in the contemporary culture.

The uniformity of early medieval civilization made temporarily possible the dominance of one form of

Christianity in western Europe. But presently an expanding cultural development in contemporary life produced new variations. This historical process gained fresh momentum with the passing of the centuries and the spread of settlements to the new world. Living persons, who cherished and perpetuated the Christian religion, participated in this variegated expansion. Variety need not cause surprise. History made just this type of Christianity to function effectively in this kind of a world. Attempts to restore uniformity, except as they follow unifying processes in contemporary culture, are sure to prove artificial, if not actually disastrous.

Nothing remains permanently stagnant in the ever flowing historical stream of life, and religion necessarily partakes of this fluidity. It moves with the current both when the water flows smoothly and when it plunges violently over a rocky terrain. There is a popular but entirely erroneous notion that the stream of religion ought always to show only a placid surface. But history proves this idea false. Times of stress provide religion its greatest opportunities for growth and functional efficiency. When we speak fearfully of "menacing crises," we may forget that they have always been the leaven generating new vitality in the inert mass of outworn tradition.

History teaches us that Christianity thrives on crises. At the very outset opposition, culminating in savage outbursts of persecution, may have seemed to place insurmountable barriers in the way of Christian success. No more critical times could be imagined. The struggle endured, not for one year or one decade, but intermittently for three centuries. And then, a hundred years after Tertullian had remarked that the blood of Christians is the seed of the church, history made good his pronouncement. Time and again the state of the world has seemed so hopeless that Christians have despaired of its continuance. But ultimately the darkest clouds have always passed away and Christians of the new day have continued to carry on with renewed efficiency. Crises furnish the occasion for change, movement, and a fresh attack by a still further-disciplined generation upon both old and new problems. As long as religion continues to stem from life itself, we may trust our descendants to learn for themselves to live effectively in their particular sort of habitable world. History will continue to generate religion.

The process of development in Christianity has now been operating for nineteen hundred years, until today there is a vast accumulation of historical deposits that tend to obscure the demand for creative living under new conditions. We are more concerned to conserve what has crystallized upon the pages of the past than to effect the release of new energy for future tasks. We would enjoy the results of previous effort rather than undertake new conquests. History is an excellent corrective for this error. It enables us to distinguish between Christianity as a vital religious movement maintained by the activities of real people and those numerous and important by-products of the movement that have acquired a static existence in days gone by. Too often these subsidiary items are mistaken for the parent-force that gave them birth.

The Bible is one of those products of religion that tend to assume the role of creator. The historian knows that the Bible is an incidental outgrowth of the Hebrew and Christian religions over a thousand-year period. Thus it is a source of information about these religions at successive stages in their career. But it did not generate them; they generated it. It was the product of the strenuous action and thinking of many different religious persons who lived aggressively in many different situations. We find it instructive and inspiring to make their acquaintance, but we abuse them when we assume that their accomplishments have left us a finished product simply to be appropriated rather than a developing religion demanding continuity of creative effort on the part of each new generation of adherents. To treat the Bible as though it were the one authentic deposit of religion in its final form—a body of revelation once for all delivered to the saints—is to substitute a part for the whole and to mistake one crop of fruit for the generative energy that reproduces the harvest in successive seasons.

The very idea of revelation is a seductive concept apt to prove misleading unless viewed in the light of history. Then it will be noted that revelation is always mediated through human persons who entertain their religious convictions with so much assurance that their words seem to them, or to their successors, to be the very utterance of the Deity. Different persons may attain this conviction in different ways. In some instances ecstasy may be the mediating agent; for others it may be the voice of conscience responding to a lively ethical urge, or an overwhelming sense of wonder in contemplating nature, or a reverence for the orderly operations of human reason in pursuit of the mind of God, or a mystical susceptibility to the whispers of a still small voice within the human spirit. Whatever the medium of communication may be, the student of history knows that revelation is to be accredited only as the sincere conviction of the religious person who sponsors the allegedly revealed truth.

These religious convictions are historical deposits whose importance for later times depends upon their degree of correspondence with the convictions engendered by the religious living of subsequent ages. The apprehension of revelation is always an act of man, and the attempt to ascribe absolute validity to revelation is a futile effort so long as the items revealed have to be strained through the mind of the human medium. Revelation is thus only what every sincere religious man believes to be divine truth, and it is capable of as much variation as marks the life and thinking of different persons living under different conditions in the various periods of history. While it remains an experiential attainment of each man's vital religion, it continues to have significance for him, but it becomes a hindrance to creative religious living by others when it is set up as a norm for blind obedience or is exploited as an authority never to be revised in later times.

The revelation that really endures is only that which repeats itself in the experience of actual persons as they pursue their respective paths in life. It is the measure in which they are severally conscious of divine guidance. To profess allegiance to an external authority, whose validity one has not tested for one's self, is to be content with religion at second hand. As a historical phenomenon, revelation, like life itself, is a fluid term and subject to the same processes of change that condition all human living. God has not decreed that knowledge of himself should be forced upon men beyond their powers of comprehension at any specific stage in their cultural development.

Institutions are another product of historical religion. The personnel of a religious group has to renew itself about every quarter-century, and in this process the element of permanence is always at stake. Consequently, religions that seek to survive must early give attention to the establishment of some form of institutional machinery designed to standardize conduct and insure continuity. Quickly specific types of organization emerge. Custom establishes one or another brand of polity. Officials acquire recognition; sacred seasons become fixed; definite forms of ritual gain currency; and the total operations of the new institution assume supreme validity on their own account. Their original functional value as products of religion is supplanted by the notion that to perform these operations is to generate religion. Once again the child assumes the role of parent.

When the historian grasps this subtle fact, he will not be greatly agitated over the question of which type of ecclesiastical institution is authentic. Indeed, each is authentic in the sense that at some time and for certain groups in specific situations it served the purpose for which it was designed. Its functional efficiency is the measure of its worth. If the cause of religion is best aided in one setting by an episcopally organized church, but in other settings a presbyterial or a congregational polity operates most effectively, each form justifies itself by its works. One does not acquire religion by joining a certain type of church. Religion comes first, and church membership follows as a result, when one is dealing with the phenomenon of voluntary action. The church is the mechanism that we employ to nourish the interest, direct the energy, and channel toward useful ends the activities of religious people. This is the purpose for which historical Christianity created the church.

Similarly, religious dogma is a product of history. It is true that one cannot be religious without possessing strong convictions regarding the value of a specific way of life. But one who follows through the historical process by which the creeds of the different churches originated and survived cannot regard these formulas as other than man-made pronouncements. Yet this is the very fact that makes them significant. They represent the earnest efforts of religious people at different stages of culture, and in their respective environments, to frame explicit definitions of their faith. The result has varied from time to time, keeping step with the knowledge and experience of Christian people. And history teaches us that the process will still continue so long as each new generation takes seriously the question of proper religious opinions. But we must remember that no creed has any validity beyond its power to win the assent of the believer.

Historical religion has also stressed ethics; it has imposed rigid rules upon the living of its disciples. While the standards for personal conduct are usually absolute in theory, they have, as a matter of fact, been highly relative in practice. Opinions about right and wrong show the same variable character that marks other historical phenomena. Loyalty to conscience may be strenuously maintained, but conscience itself is tutored by heritage and circumstance. Ethical ideals are formulated differently by different persons in varying situations. Religious history does not offer a single rule for moral action but a series of urges that men may follow only to discover new demands awaiting them in days to come. Ethical excellence is not something that can be fully acquired at a specific moment and thereafter enjoyed without disturbance for the remainder of one's days. It is rather the impulse to discover and pursue the correct way of life in each new situation that emerges on every fresh horizon of the future.

Christianity has always aimed to generate worthy

character. Rules by which the good man will regulate his thought and action have often been formulated. But a life of mechanical conformity to rules, however excellent they may be, is an inadequate test of virtue. Conformity may be only the result of fear or indolence due to utter lack of initiative. One who observes rigidly current rules may have no more character than a typewriter or a motor car, each of which acts strictly according to the mechanics of its construction. The instrument cannot go astray on its own account; it is totally lacking in personal character because it has no native capacity for choosing between good and evil. The operator is the one who perverts the machine; it is he who possesses or lacks character.

The quality of the motive behind the act, rather than the rule followed in its performance, is what determines character. This is a feature of life that develops with experience and is amenable to no set of fixed prescriptions. Some of the most worthy persons in religious history, impelled by the urge toward a more excellent way of life, have deliberately violated the currently established regulations for conduct. They saw duty in heretofore uncharted areas of action which they undertook to explore at the behest of an irrepressible inner urge. They built character afresh under the pressure of evolving experience. Character itself is a product of religious living; it is still in the process of being made and remade by the developing course of history.

[174]

C. THE PROBLEM OF HUMAN ACTIVISM

The Christian movement, viewed historically, is ultimately an evolving process of life that has been sponsored by actual people during the past nineteen hundred years. The course of the development still continues and will endure so long as history remains in the making. When viewed in the light of the innumerable years that stretch away into the distant future, it may well be that Christianity has not yet passed beyond its early childhood. The changes it may undergo during the next two thousand years, or during the next ten thousand, and the uncounted centuries that lie beyond, cannot be forecast with certainty. But no sober student of history can doubt that changes will occur in the future as in the past. Otherwise Christianity will scarcely endure. Should it harden to the point where it loses all power of responding to the demands of new experience or of meeting life on the realistic level of each new day, then it will have to be abandoned to the scrap pile of evolving civilization.

The perpetuation of Christianity, or of religion by whatever name it may be called, is a human responsibility. Knowledge of God can increase in the world only as men develop keener powers of comprehending the Divine Presence. The mind of the Deity remains unknown until historical persons have acquired the capacity for peering behind the veil of material existence to catch fresh glimpses of spiritual reality. Also, the suppression of evil and the dominance of good wait upon human action. There is no progress without strenuous labor and rigidly imposed self-discipline. Effective ethical obligations must, in the last analysis, be a recognition of duties demanded by man's own enlightened spirit. The intelligence of his choices, the sincerity of his will, and the diligence of his devotion to the noblest ideals that he has learned how to apprehend condition the possibility of all religious improvement. Historical religion survives by being embodied in the experience and activity of actual persons living in specific situations within one or another area of the earth's surface. Thus religious living is definitely a human task. It always has been so in the past, and it must ever continue to be such in the future.

The making of religious history is a heavy responsibility to place upon mankind. Our ideals constantly outrun our accomplishments, and this experience prompts us to doubt our competence for the task in hand. Furthermore, we transfer this same inability to all future generations and predict failure before effort has begun. The task seems beyond human power to perform. Awareness of impending failure becomes especially acute in periods of social disruption that threaten to submerge past moral and spiritual values. Then we begin to talk of bewildering crises that seem to menace the very survival of religion.

There are two typical ways of meeting crises in religion. One procedure, rather popular in some quarters today, declares that human efforts to attain religious excellence are totally vain. Religion, unlike other phases of human culture, is said not to be a result of man's struggle to rise to higher wisdom and righteousness. We are told that in the sphere of religion man is utterly incompetent. His failure consists in having attempted a task that lies wholly outside his province. It is a matter that concerns God only. And, since he is not involved in the imperfections and misadventures of the human order of being, one must invent for him another sphere of action beyond the range of human history. Thus arises the twofold division into secular and sacred history. The former occurs on the observable level, but the latter lies outside of and above the world of normal human knowledge. Hence it can be made to assume characteristics and discharge functions utterly incapable of being tested by the criteria of actual experience. Men are relieved of the obligation to solve crises by handing the task over to the Almighty.

Sacred history is a fertile field for producing unverifiable affirmations of faith. In this supernatural area there is no evolution, no gradual unfolding of wisdom, no testing to distinguish between good and evil, no uncertainty or tentativeness about alleged truth. All is complete, final, and absolute in theory. Men are incapable of penetrating this hypothetical upper world, but some rays of light have streamed down thence by means of revelation. This impinges upon men from without; it must not be made a product of their personal religious growth. Its content is factual, static, and supernaturally valid. It is to be implicitly accepted rather than tested in the mundane process of creative religious living within the scope of secular history.

This type of thinking has often emerged at critical periods in the past. It is not surprising that it should have been revived in recent times to console us for our failure to make the ideals of religion triumphant in modern society. In a period of severe stress it is comforting to learn that we are not charged with the task of redeeming the world by a more strenuous process of our own living on the mundane level. We are accused of looking too much to the state of this real world without paying sufficient regard to the imagined world of sacred history. Affirmations about revealed truth are said to be more important than experimental quests for wisdom; a declaration of belief in God is far more virtuous than an attempted life of daily fellowship with him. For man to confess his utter worthlessness in the sight of God is more commendable than any effort he may make to be "perfect as the Heavenly Father is perfect." Life upon the plane of human history has no positive religious content apart from the acceptance of allegedly revealed truth handed down from God. And crises are not to be resolved by men but are to be accepted simply as evidence of the divine judgment and are to be endured until God intervenes to bring the present temporal order to a close.

Thus temporal history loses its religious significance. Human activism in pursuit of righteousness is a misdirected effort, and man's struggle to shape life from age to age under the direction of God immanent in the present world is pure folly. The essential thing in religion is to assert convictions rather than to pursue a way of life. This is the whole duty of man. When he has affirmed his faith, he has performed his part in the religious sphere. He leaves to God the solution of the moral and spiritual problems that perplex men who are too ready to meddle in God's government of the world.

Today this mode of thinking has invaded several areas of our modern life. Under the leadership of Karl Barth it has engaged the favorable attention of many theologians. It has cast its restraining shadow over regions where men formerly pursued the ideals of a vigorous social gospel. And still more recently it has aroused debate in the field of religious education. It would protest against the effort to induce creative religious living by the process of education and would substitute therefor a program of authoritative indoctrination. And how is the doctrine to be validated? Only by resort to a theoretical sphere of alleged revelation lying outside the realm of specifically human history. On this program the past in human experience has no essentially constructive religious meaning. It is merely an interregnum that temporarily interrupts the course of sacred history.

The second way of dealing with critical situations rejects outright the program of escape to the hypothetical world of sacred history. Instead of shifting responsibility to God, men steel themselves for more strenuous efforts. They study human history more diligently to ascertain the secrets of failure or success in the past and thus to increase wisdom for future conduct. When they take seriously the story of the past, they become keenly aware of the fact that crises can never be ignored with impunity; they must always be resolved by effort. Confronted by mounting difficulties, there is only one sensible course open to men. They must assume larger responsibilities and increase their efforts. They must define more intelligently the methods to be employed and the ideals to be realized in further attempts to bring in the Kingdom of God. The struggle to comprehend the divine will must be more earnestly pursued, and there must be a greater devotion to the task of making religion a vital reality for the world of today and tomorrow.

There is a pious ring about the old slogan that calamity is God's judgment upon humans for their sins. At an earlier period in the history of civilization it was appropriate to envisage a righteous God in the role of an offended monarch executing judgment upon his disobedient subjects. But today the imagery lacks verisimilitude. Modern men depose the monarchical despot and assume responsibility for determining their own political destiny. And in the area of religion, good and evil are seen to be products of human action rather than donations or punishments supernaturally bestowed or imposed by the hand of Deity. Man has been created so truly in the image of God that human action is free to follow whatever course it may choose.

By experience man learns that pursuit of evil brings ultimate disaster, and by the same token he also learns that deliverance from evil comes only through his further determination to pursue good.

Past defeats are simply a challenge to fresh endeavor. If they were divine chastisements, it would be a sin to try to avoid them; and, if the judge acted fairly, he would punish the actual persons who committed the offense. But in the processes of history one generation's mistakes saddle troubles upon the children, while the sinning ancestors escape scot-free. In primitive times one could say that the iniquity of the fathers was visited upon the children to the third and fourth generation. In those days it was a vengeful Deity whom men revered, but that conception can no longer be tolerated where a modern sense of justice prevails. The "sinners" who framed the Treaty of Versailles, to take a familiar illustration, have pretty generally escaped the consequences of their "crime." Most of them had disappeared from the stage before World War II broke out, and such as were still living were safely beyond the military age. Thus they evaded the divine punishment that fell upon their innocent descendants who were drafted for war. Can we believe that God is so arbitrary a monarch, or so vindictive a feudal noble, that he could find satisfaction in executing punishment upon guiltless sons and daughters of sinful parents who are peacefully reposing in their tombs? Calamity is not a divine judgment but is the natural consequence of failure to embrace opportunity.

And the only remedy for the resulting trouble is wiser action and more persistent endeavor. The decision and the responsibility have been left with man. That fact makes him a fellow-worker with Deity in founding the Kingdom of God on earth.

The religious man of today may derive from the past a rich fund of wisdom regarding the discharge of his responsibility in the present and the future. By this means he becomes fully aware of the essential nature of the Christian enterprise. It is the continued story of religious living on the part of real people who, from first to last, have constituted the membership of the movement. Under the impact of varied social contacts they have chosen, from time to time, that course of procedure which seemed to them best suited to secure and preserve the inheritances, the ideals, and the attainments which appealed most strongly to their sense of worth. As the movement grew, the stream of time has thrown up and borne along on its surface, or left stranded along its shores, various items of ritual practice, forms of organization, and bodies of formulated doctrine. Thus the complex organization called the "church" has come into being, and its significance in the present cultural situation can be understood only as one becomes familiar with the process of its development. Attempts to pull down out of the sky the ideal pattern of a church triumphant that will some day supplant the terrestrial church militant has been a favorite sport among some theologians; but nobody ever saw or ever will see a real church on earth that is not a product of the human struggle to establish an institution that will serve the religious interests of its members.

The organized Christian movement of today, even when taken in all its varied aspects, is seen to be no artificial and ephemeral structure. Rather, it is the outcome of nineteen centuries of human endeavor to make concrete and effective in institutional forms the results of men's efforts to realize for themselves and their successors their highest conceivable spiritual values. An institution of this character will not readily consent to be forgotten or reformed; its roots penetrate too deeply into the soil of humanity's past. It is futile to talk about an ideal church when the only church that history knows, or ever can know, is one that men themselves make—men with passions, impulses, capacities for spiritual attainment, and inclinations toward evil and good, such as have been manifested in the past. The church of the future that arises on the human plane will have to be constructed out of the same type of brick and mortar that has gone into its structure in days gone by. What the church will be, or may be, tomorrow cannot be intelligently forecast by one who is unfamiliar with the course of its history during the previous stages of its career.

At the same time, heritages from the past will justify their right to survive only by the measure of their functional value in the experience of the continuing Christian society. The pious soul who insists that what was good enough for her grandmother is good enough for her is quite within her rights if she actually finds a full measure of satisfaction in her strict adherence to tradition. One who has read history wisely will have discovered that the heart of the Christian society is the religious living of its personnel, and that inherited features—whether in the form of creeds, rites, or ethical precepts—which are still functioning effectively in maintaining spiritual quests may not be tampered with lightly. Not until the demand for change emerges within the experience of the individual or the group does the problem of adjustment become acute, and at that point man must assume responsibility for its solution. He must think and act his way to new levels of religious knowledge and attainment.

Acquaintance with history will also save one from wasting energy on untimely issues. When the theory of normativeness has been set aside, one will not seek to perpetuate items in the Christian heritage that no longer integrate themselves vitally with the world of modern times. Occasionally much energy has been expended in well-meaning efforts to refloat on the stream of life the stranded hulk of some worn-out phase of belief or ritual. Perhaps it was the rite of foot-washing, or premillennial teaching, that was to be reinstated. Each of these items had its place in historic Christianity and was significant in its original setting, but both are quite out of place in a society where different footwear is used and where catastrophe is no longer in vogue as a philosophy of history.

The question of preserving or discarding historical heritages is only a secondary problem; more fundamental is the task of constructive and creative activity. This is the chief responsibility of the religious man of today and tomorrow. He is charged with the duty of bringing into existence a vital Christianity for the new day. As he reads history, he discovers that each generation of Christians, although rightful heir to all that has gone before, has also been genuinely the maker of the specific Christianity of its own age. In the presence of new persons, new environments, new experience, and new knowledge Christianity is being continually reborn to newness of life under the leadership of vigorous individuals. One readily discovers that leaders in the past, if they have been leaders in fact, accomplished their task through a fresh impact upon the life of their own age and through devotion to new loyalties forged directly out of their most immediate and deepest experiences. Although they were commonly at one with their contemporaries in holding to the traditional theory of a normative past, authenticated by special revelation, they nevertheless gave most immediate heed to the promptings of the still small voice speaking within their own souls as they confronted new crises in living.

No revelation from the past can transcend the imperious command of present duty. The religious man reads the whole story of Christianity's career as a record of human and divine relations on the terrestrial plane where the God of history is simply the God of man's experience—the continuing Christian experience of all the centuries, but no less the experience of those who live today. The historian finds no occasion for assuming that God is less real and immediate in the life of today than he was in that of yesterday. In this conviction there is ample justification for believing that the Christianity of the future will triumph over new difficulties with the same vital energy that it has always displayed in the past. It is of the very nature of Christianity, as a movement still in the making, that the quest for righteousness should renew and realize itself afresh with each new stage of cultural evolution experienced by mankind.

Herein lies the great challenge to Christians who face the crises of the present hour. They are summoned to serve a cause that stands for moral and spiritual progress in days when the going is most difficult. They must forge ahead, however hard may be the way. The past is theirs in so far as it serves their needs, but they are never its bondservants. They will be but little better than blind guides of the blind if they are content to be mere echoes of a bygone age. Instead, they are called to be high priests of tomorrow's spiritual order and seekers after a new righteousness that will not attain its goal until it aspires to exceed the righteousness of the yesterdays.

These are the lessons that we learn from our study of the past. Religious living is a creative process in the growth of human persons consciously striving to subject their material existence to their moral and spiritual ideals. These ideals develop with enlarging experience as this is acquired from history and from current life. Religion, like every other phase of human culture, is a process of evolutionary growth. Man's knowledge of God, like all other human wisdom, has to be attained by effort and increases according to the intensity with which it is pursued.

Also, man must struggle to overcome evil with good. Age on age, the conflict will endure. The only promise of relief offered by actual history is the halting success of the human endeavor to live more devoutly and creatively with the dawn of each new day. Activism, constantly renewed and persistently pursued so long as life remains, is the royal road to victory. No man who relaxes his quest or refuses to accept his full responsibility for carrying on God's work in the world is fit for the Kingdom of Heaven on earth.

Religion today needs, not less divine guidance, but more human virility—more devotees who will vigorously respond to the challenging summons of William Pierson Merrill:

> Rise up O men of God!
>   His kingdom tarries long;
> Bring in the day of brotherhood
>   And end the night of wrong.

CHAPTER VII

GOD AND THE HISTORICAL PROCESS

CHRISTIAN philosophy has always been theistic; belief in God has been a cardinal item in all Christian thinking. But the mutual relation between God and the concrete events of man's daily living has been subject to much difference of opinion. While history reveals man's responsibility for the pursuit of truth and his quest for the attainment of spiritual values, God's participation in the active operations of the historical process is more difficult to determine.

The difficulty is twofold. In the first place, God has been so variously pictured in his relation to human events that a consistent Christian interpretation of divine action on the strictly mundane level still remains unrealized. And, secondly, evil and good are so confusingly mingled in the processes of historical evolution that any thought of God's immediate and continued activity in the affairs of men seems to menace the absolute perfection and infinite wisdom traditionally associated with the notion of the Deity.

A. VARYING PICTURES OF GOD

Why is it that men have thought of God in so many different ways? Even within historic Christianity there has been a distinct lack of uniformity in its the-istic imagery. Yet one may say that two chief tribu-taries have converged to furnish the main stream of Christian thinking about God. One of these is He-brew, and the other is Greek.

Hebrew theistic thinking was anthropomorphic; it pictured the Deity in the shape of an all-powerful man. He made a world as a man would build a machine; but he was so supremely potent that he needed only to speak his word of command and the thing was accomplished. He fashioned light and darkness; he separated the night from the day; he gave shape to each living creature on land and in the sea and the air; and he created human beings to render him worshipful obedience. The whole fabricated universe was subject to his mighty will, even as a man maintains mastery over the things that he has made.

Like a man toying with the playthings he has cre-ated, God continued to manifest his interest in the world by means of unusual displays in connection with the phenomena of nature. When he uttered his voice, the earth trembled. He clothed himself in the gar-ments of lightning, thunder, and hurricane. He purged the sinful earth with an overwhelming flood and then set a rainbow in the sky as a pledge against any repeti-tion of the disaster. But presently he rained down brimstone and fire from heaven to destroy the wicked Sodom and Gomorrah. As his anger could blaze out in fierce fury, so his favor could be procured by the covenanted obedience of the faithful Abraham. God was the divine tradesman who bargained for a chosen people's loyalty and thus secured for himself a group of worshipers to do him honor.

God remained the supernatural guardian over his chosen race throughout the entire course of its history. He miraculously insured descendants for Abraham; he directed their course into Egypt; and he displayed his mastery over nature's laws when he held back the waters of the Red Sea to permit the fleeing Hebrews to pass over on dry land. During their wanderings in the wilderness he quenched their thirst by causing water to spurt out of a rock, and he fed them with manna from heaven. He provided them with a pillar of cloud by day and a pillar of fire by night to mark their course toward the Promised Land. And when they reached their destination, he cleared the way for their entry by causing the walls of Jericho to crumble at their approach.

God remained the guardian of the Hebrew social order throughout the entire course of its career in the land of Canaan. On numerous occasions he was thought to have intervened to protect and order his people's way of life. He initiated every new stage in their proper social evolution, and he placed impediments in the way when they strayed into forbidden paths. He shaped their political institutions, although they were often slow to perceive his will. He authenticated their moral laws, even dictating to Moses the elemental principles of their ethical system. Their religious rites and customs were derived from the same divine source. God's decrees determined right and wrong, and to obey his perfect law insured piety, wisdom, and rejoicing of heart. In every sphere of activity God was pictured as the wisest, most righteous, and all-powerful superman presiding over the destinies of the descendants of Abraham.

Like the head of a human family, God exercised his authority over the people of his choice. He provided them with the means of subsistence; he insured their survival by blessing their women with fertility; and he required an obedience such as a father demanded of the members of an ideal household. Especially was the pious man accounted a son of God, but the whole Hebrew race were his rightful children, over whom he kept watch with sleepless solicitude. When they were obedient, he rewarded them with blessings; but their perversities were requited with afflictions. Yet he had a father's compassion for his erring children; and, like a human parent, he pitied them in their misfortunes. In superhuman perfection God indulged the same emotions that marked the life of man; he approved the obedient, he punished the sinner, he lamented the perversity of the recalcitrant, and he loved the members of his family with an abiding affection.

Over the entire range of their theistic thinking the Hebrews employed pictorial imagery to describe how God felt and acted. Since they were content to think of him in terms of manlike conduct on the supernatural level, they never indulged in abstract speculation regarding the constitution of his person. In other words, their method was mythological in the best sense of that term. They trusted to descriptive narrative to convey truth, and so made no effort to supply a metaphysical justification of the pictorial imagery used to describe the conduct and character of God. He remained a strictly anthropomorphic being. Faith rested on the vivid portrayal of divine action; it needed no support from the philosopher's arguments.

The first Christians in Palestine pictured God in thoroughly Hebrew fashion. He was the heroic performer of mighty deeds who held sovereign sway over the world. Although his all-wise designs were beyond full human comprehension, it was assumed that the advocates of the new religious movement understood them best. Christians regarded themselves in a special sense as children of this supreme Heavenly Father. Yet for the time being he was much concerned with the good of all mankind, and his new devotees had a keen sense of their responsibility to spread their gospel abroad. Mercy and justice both remained operative as divine attributes during the period of transition to an early state of the world when God, either directly or by means of the mediation of Christ, would inaugurate a new age in which his patience with sinners would end in their final destruction. In the meantime Christians enjoyed miraculous displays of heavenly favor in anticipation of the blessings awaiting them in the age to come.

This theistic imagery of the early Christians was characteristically Hebraic. God was dramatically pictured as a superman acting on behalf of the members of the Christian society. He was worshiped and obeyed because of the conviction produced by the vivid manner in which he was portrayed. His supremacy and power were exhibited "mythologically," and the description was so convincing that it did not need to be supplemented by any rigidly logical proof. The anthropomorphic realism was self-sufficient.

When Christianity spread beyond Palestine, where it soon began to receive Gentiles into its membership, it found anthropomorphic imagery extravagantly employed to describe the activities of various Greek and Roman deities. At the outset Christians did not question the propriety of portraying the Deity as a supernatural man. Instead, they claimed exclusive rights to the procedure as they applied it to the Hebrew God of the Old Testament, with whom the figure of the risen Christ was now associated in the heavenly sphere. All gentile divinities were declared to be evil demons bent upon hindering or perverting the Christian cause. God and Christ as revered by Christians now took over all beneficent supernatural functions, while the demons continued to practice their malevolent designs. But, since Christianity was sure to succeed, the demons were destined for ultimate destruction. God and Christ were supernatural powers whose triumph was depicted in the same type of anthropomorphic imagery to which the Gentiles had long been accustomed. The current mythology was Christianized by being reformed and restricted to the God of the Old Testament

[193]

and the exalted Christ of Christian tradition. Their supernatural activities were vividly described as the only necessary means of producing conviction and securing converts.

After Christianity had been in gentile lands for about a hundred years, it began to attract a few Greek philosophers, who introduced a new type of theistic language. For several centuries Greek thinkers had been protesting against the folly of depicting the Deity in human form. Tradition reports that Xenophanes of Elia in the sixth century before Christ had charged Homer and Hesiod with attributing to the gods conduct that would disgrace respectable men. Even to picture gods as good men was also ridiculous, for if animals had hands and could carve images each would make his god to look like his idealized self. One who would truly conceive of the Deity must think in terms of more abstract and nonhuman imagery. As Xenophanes expressed it, "God is all sight, all mind, all ear, and without effort rules everything by thought." Thus God was an abstraction to be apprehended by the mind rather than an individual entity to be seen by an imaginary physical eye.

About the same time Heraclitus of Ephesus propounded another type of theistic thinking that was destined to exert a wide influence. He declared the universe to be in constant motion under the control of an all-pervading reason. This reason, being itself the ultimate substance of the universe as well as the force generating its motion, was God. It was called the eternal "Logos," the divine rational principle, which constituted both the substance of the living universe and the process by which it was maintained. God was not an abstraction, as Xenophanes had seemed to hold, but a cosmic rational energy existing in material form. He and the universe were inseparable, contemporaneous, and coequal. This was characteristic Stoic teaching.

The Platonic division of the universe into a duality of incorporeal ideas and material substance made it possible to think of God as a spiritual entity free from the limitations of a material being and yet possessed of qualities like truth and beauty and goodness that were in reality abstractions of human virtues. God and the world of matter could now be conceived of as separate entities, and the relation between them could be maintained in terms of an earthly approximation to the inimitable heavenly pattern. By positing a dualism of the real and the ideal world and locating the Deity in the latter, one freed God of all anthropomorphic limitations; yet he remained a model for all virtuous conduct and thinking on the part of man. Since God no longer belonged to the physical world but was a being beyond material reality, knowledge of him could be acquired only by means of metaphysical speculation. Thus, among Greek intellectuals philosophy displaced mythology as a way of acquiring knowledge of God, and thereby he was removed from immediate contact with the world of men and things.

When Greek philosophers came into Christianity,

they began the process of transforming the character-istically anthropomorphic God of Hebrew imagery into a figure metaphysically more respectable. He could not be allowed to have those intimate contacts with the material world that the mythological repre-sentation demanded. This tendency came to clear ex-pression in the Christian philosophy of Justin Martyr soon after the middle of the second century. His Pla-tonic heritage compelled Justin to make the Christian God a fully transcendent being. He was invisible to human eyes, indescribable in the language of man, in-capable of dwelling in any one place, quick to behold and quick to hear, although having neither eyes nor ears, and possessed of incomprehensible might. He was encumbered by none of the limitations that be-longed to men; nor did he move about after the man-ner of a human being. Instead, he was a transcendent abstraction, almighty in power and infinite in wisdom.

Under the influence of Platonic idealism among in-tellectually inclined Christians their God was com-pelled to withdraw from the concrete world of histori-cal happenings. But the world was not left without divine care. Christian philosophers took over the Sto-ic conception of the permeating Logos, individualizing it in the person of Christ, who was said to have func-tioned as God's mediator, really a "second God," all through the course of the world's history. Thus the Old Testament Deity became a God in dignified repose, while Christ had been God in action from before the foundation of the world. And still the theologians in-

sisted that there were not two gods but only one.
There was no other way in which they could reconcile
the fact that Christianity's philosophical converts had
devised for the new religion a metaphysical Deity
while it had inherited an anthropomorphic one from
its Hebrew predecessors. And each type of thinking
served too useful a purpose to allow it to be discarded.

After Christianity had become the recognized religion of the Roman state and its God had been assigned
the task of furnishing divine protection to all of society, its theistic imagery became more definitely im-
perialistic. Stress was laid upon the supreme authority
of God's will and the absolute obedience required of
men. Neoplatonism, the latest philosophy to arise
in the ancient world, made God absolute being, while
political imagery gave him almighty will. And so Augustine believed both the anger and the grace of God
to be irresistible; "even with the very wills of men
he does what he will when he will." Still later, Aristotelian philosophy, which made God the "unmoved
mover," was introduced into Christianity by Thomas
Aquinas. But this motive power had operated in the
creation of the universe rather than in the current
processes of contemporary history. God was pure ac-
tuality, absolutely incorporeal, the maintenance of
whose dignity and authority was the chief end of human existence.

The general trend of Greek philosophy's influence
upon Christian thinking, whether Platonic, Aristotelian, or Neoplatonic, was to remove God beyond the

human sphere and thus to eliminate him from immediate participation in the ordinary affairs of mankind. Only where the Stoic heritage survived could the doctrine of divine immanence be retained. But the average Christian was not a philosopher. He really had little or no concern with metaphysical representations of the Deity. The theologians might bitterly debate questions of theistic speculation, but the rank and file of Christians were quite satisfied with the anthropomorphic God of popular faith. They believed in a divine power that was thought to be always near at hand and able, if he so willed, to order the events of each man's day in a miraculous manner.

Christian thinkers dealt in a similar manner with the problem of evil. When the philosophers defined the Deity in the abstract terms of omnipotence and holiness, he was necessarily excluded from intimate participation in the affairs of a world where both evil and good were pervasively intermingled. If evil originated with God, that fact would seem to deny his holiness; and, if it existed in spite of his will to the contrary, that fact seemed to impair his omnipotence. How could God stand related to a historical process in which evil and good were integral factors? Varying answers to this question were proposed.

The mythological type of answer permitted evils to emanate from God himself; they were punishments inflicted by him upon those who disobeyed his commands. The Hebrews often interpreted their sufferings in the light of this theory of divine retribution. But they also asked the more ultimate question of why man was disposed to go astray. One typical reply was that evil also had a supernatural origin. It was said to proceed from a satanic source opposed to God and intent upon the complete degradation of man. Thus the conflict between good and evil was a battle between two supernatural forces—God and Satan. While the historical process endured, the strife still continued; but in the end God would be triumphant, and righteous men would share in his victory over the prince of evil. This was the "mythological" way of solving the problem of evil, and it quite satisfied the mental demands of the ordinary Christian.

Christian philosophers, however, attempted a metaphysical explanation of the age-old problem. Stoic speculation had identified God so closely with the material world that all of nature's operations had to be essentially good. Sometimes men in their own foolishness did wicked deeds, but God so overruled even their perversities that ultimately everything worked together for good. Since the seat of evil was human ignorance, discipline in philosophical understanding of the Stoic system of thinking was the panacea for all the ills of the world. A few Christian philosophers in the earlier days of the movement's history were disposed to view evil somewhat after the Stoic manner, but the Stoic's strenuous self-therapy never entered widely into Christian thinking.

The dualism of Plato, with his ideal world of incorporeal reality and his lower world of material existences, proved more congenial to the Christian mind. Evil could be assigned its locus in matter while the incorporeal sphere remained totally good. And the problem of evil was to be solved by rescuing the souls of men from bondage to materiality, just as God had escaped any contact with evil by belonging wholly to the incorporeal realm. If matter were not an actual source of evil, it was at least an impediment to good on the level of mundane existence. But God was quite removed from the scene himself, and he had provided through Christ an adequate means of rescuing the souls of men from their earthly entanglements.

These varying pictures of God, moving from the mythical to the metaphysical type, tended to push him farther and farther away from the operations of the daily historical process. As he was transported beyond the world of historical reality into the hypothetical world created by philosophical speculation, he gradually lost his human features, interests, and emotions. Then the character and functions of God could be defined before consulting history. The Deity of the philosophers was never a product of historical research but was a figure superimposed from without upon the events of history. The historical process itself either was completely ignored or else was stretched to fit the prescribed theistic pattern.

B. HISTORY AND THE SCIENTIFIC WORLD VIEW

It may be that knowledge of God can best be ascertained by means of philosophical speculation. The

[200]

study of history does not aim to yield metaphysical truth; nor does it offer itself as a substitute for philosophical inquiry. It has no tools with which to discover esoteric wisdom beyond the plain realities of recoverable events. It can record the signs of the times and tell us how men have acted or what they have believed, but it hesitates to read into events meanings that are too obscure to be seen by the processes of normal observation. On the other hand, the philosopher's quest for wisdom travels the exalted highway of logical argument and rational inference to a knowledge of things unseen, while the historian wanders amid the lowlands of time and human happenings. Perhaps travelers upon this lower route may not expect to attain full knowledge of God. In any event, it should be clearly recognized that their attempt must suffer from very definite limitations.

What can the historian, as historian, hope to learn about God from the observable course of human events on the purely natural level? Historical inquiry has today become a scientific quest that may not with propriety call upon supernatural or experimentally unverifiable forces to account for human happenings. Therefore, it must refrain from seeking to discover God either in anthropomorphic imagery or in metaphysical speculation. Both of these areas of activity are forbidden to the student of history in his role as historian; he must deal only with the orderly universe of modern science. And, since science is commonly thought to be purely a quest for knowledge of nature,

[201]

it might be supposed to exclude the very possibility of learning anything about God as long as one adheres to a scientific view of the world. Are not religion and science incompatibles?

Any attempt to synthesize the Christian religion and modern scientific thinking is fraught with many difficulties. Sometimes Christianity has so defined its goals as to make their attainment in the world of nature impossible. It seeks to know a God who is said to transcend the bounds of human knowledge. It adores as creator and sustainer of the universe a being whom it has never seen and whose form is thought to be inaccessible to human eyes. It strives to effect communion between finite creatures and God, while at the same time it declares him to be an incomprehensibly infinite spirit. It would shape human conduct and thinking in accordance with a divine pattern the full measure of which it declares itself incapable of apprehending. It preaches that men should be perfect as the Father in heaven is perfect, and yet it affirms that the Supreme Deity alone can be truly holy, righteous, and good. In short, this type of Christianity is concerned with imponderables beyond whose portals it ever vainly strives to pass, while science assumes that the knowledge after which it seeks is fully knowable.

On the other hand, historical Christianity has also proposed to tell people just what they should believe and how they should act under all of the contingencies of life. There has been a mounting urge within the Christian movement to specify allegedly valid doctrines, to formulate binding ethical codes, and to prescribe rules and ceremonies for correct ecclesiastical procedure. Under the impulsion to furnish an authoritative answer to all human questions, Christian theologians have described the origin and constitution of the universe; they have defined the nature, mission, and destiny of man; they have given us a detailed outline of the Deity's program for dealing with mortals; and they have provided elaborate instructions for the direction of all activities that are thought to count for righteousness.

It was entirely natural that the older theologians should claim to possess final knowledge about concrete phenomena in the natural realm of the world and man. Since it was assumed that God himself had authorized their opinions, any person who deviated from them was a menace alike to God and man. This state of mind had thoroughly crystallized centuries before science began its distinctive quest for knowledge of the physical world. Theology had pre-empted every area of opinion long before Galileo, Kepler, Newton, and their more modern successors in the field of scientific research had appeared upon the scene. It was inevitable that there should have been at the start a bitter struggle between traditional theology and the new natural science. But that conflict is now a thing of the past. Today all religious people who lay any claim to culture and education accept without reserve the scientific interpretation of the natural world, although they may feel somewhat hesitant about the propriety of its application in the field of religion.

The scientific historian cannot allow himself to share even this measure of reserve. Of course, one must not make religion identical with any specific form of theological dogma that has been formulated in past ages. Science is a quest for new knowledge, which, when it is acquired, must be allowed to displace or supplement even the most revered dogmas in every area of cultural life. What men have thought about God in the past may not readily conform to the findings of modern science, but that fact does not mean that belief in God has to be abandoned. Traditional doctrines may lose prestige, but the truth they were designed to convey and the urges that called them into being may take on a new imperiousness under the impulsion of modern scientific inquiry. While science has discredited some of the older forms of theological definition, it has, at the same time, provided a vaster perspective and a surer footing from which to approach some of the perennial concerns of religion.

The awesome reverence with which the ancient Psalmist saw in the heavens a display of God's glory and a manifestation of his handiwork is certainly not diminished by the majesty of that limitless star-spangled expanse of space revealed by the modern telescope. Religion's quest for God is not denied but is only magnified by this new experience, except for one whose spirit is so overwhelmed by immensity that he refuses to venture to explore by faith the regions of the great beyond. It is said that Laplace once remarked that he had swept the heavens with his telescope and had found no God, to which one of his critics replied that he might have swept the kitchen with a broom and had the same result. Religion calls for the outreach of the human spirit into the unfathomable depths of the cosmos. If one refuses this venture, he can hardly share the uplift of him who, though compelled to turn back in futility from his quest, is still able to perceive the glory of God in the new heavens spread out before us by the discoveries of modern astronomy. Science has not removed all of the imponderables from religion; it has only increased their immensity.

Science has also given the historian an orderly universe. Natural phenomena are linked together in an all-pervading causal nexus that never deviates from its course to please the arbitrary will of either man or God. We have learned to accept the inexorableness of natural laws. Belief in miraculous happenings accomplished by the capricious intervention of the Deity to thwart or divert nature's normal processes is no longer agreeable to our ways of thinking. But to discredit ancient faith in the miraculous does not, as used to be supposed, really cut the nerve of religion. A God who occasionally strides through the universe upsetting the universal order of which he is supposed to be the author and sustainer would seem to us a self-contradictory being. On the contrary, we would read his will more truly than we have ever done before by the knowledge which science has given us of the universal laws that permeate the cosmos.

The natural world also exhibits the presence of unlimited creative energy constantly operative in the maintenance of the universe. Plant life is perpetually renewing itself every season. In extravagant superabundance every grain of seed recreates itself many hundred fold. Every living organism is a center of creative power for reproducing in increasing measure the life of its species. All nature is shot through with the will to live and to generate life. In the conflict between life and death the defeat of the latter is clearly forecast every time one seed reproduces as many as only two of its kind. The world is overflowing with creative power. It is a living universe, and in its vital energy one may feel the presence of the living God. The older faith said that God is in his heaven and all is well with the world, but a more intensive scrutiny of the universe in which we live prompts us to say that God is in his world partaking constantly in the process of creation.

The urge of the human race toward cultural advance and the pursuit of moral and spiritual ideals suggest to the thoughtful observer that there is some force in nature inspiring these efforts. One may be content to classify them among man's spiritual quests, but the very fact of their presence attests the human kinship with the divine. Man alone has the power to cherish these high ambitions and the incentive to struggle toward their attainment. The spirit by which these efforts are inspired, their recurring persistence in the course of human history, and man's growing sensitivity to higher values, as successive generations have been tutored by time, are as clear a call of God as any attentively religious soul could wish to hear. It may not be God's voice thundering from Sinai that sounds in our ears, but only the quiet conviction of a duty to be performed or an ideal to be realized. The divine message comes from no distant age or place but is spoken by one who is ever "closer to us than breathing and nearer than hands and feet." Proximity must not be allowed to make the whisperings of God's voice less audible or his commands less impelling.

Believing that we are commissioned to work hand in hand with God in bringing his will to fulfilment among men, we cannot ignore as irrelevantly secular any knowledge or device that contributes toward the cure of souls. The knowledge that science has gathered about the working of elemental impulses in men individually and collectively, the physical and social conditions that stimulate or retard ethical behavior, and the techniques that may be most effectively employed to ameliorate distress and build character—all may be divine urges even within the commonplace experiences of daily living. These stratagems may at first seem to be only the artifices of men, but their remedial efficacy for the moral and spiritual betterment of the world bears testimony to their divine authentication.

History welcomes the prying eye of scientific inquiry even within the inner sanctuary of the human spirit where man and God meet each other in the secret chamber of the soul and where the still small voice whispers its inspirations to prophets and saints. By every natural means available the student of history would make himself familiar with every phenomenal feature in this area of religion. He would peer into the psychology of conversion. He would recognize the physical stimuli of fasting, prolonged periods of prayer, and silent meditation that attended the unique religious experiences of the great mystics of the church. He would evaluate the significance of music and art and ritual in lending solemnity and effectiveness to the rites of religious worship. He would welcome the fullest understanding of all the physical, psychological, and social phenomena that attend or can be made to contribute toward the attainment of the richest and noblest type of religious experience. And he would gladly cherish and intelligently employ every available means by which the spirit of God and the spirit of man may enter into conscious intercommunion. There are various ways by which man hears the divine voice as he makes his journey through life, and to apprehend them intelligently is to acquire a fuller knowledge of God.

The skeptic, reacting from the extravagant supernaturalism of traditional theology, has said that the only God we know is the God we make. Inverting a biblical phrase, one declares with Xenophanes that men have always made their gods in the image of man. This may be true of many or all of the pictures of the Deity that men have devised and defended. But beyond these creations of our imaginations there are the raw materials, so to speak, employed in the process of construction and the incentives that prompt us to create the imagery. The pictures, varying in form and quality, may be of our making; but the urge to produce and the elemental stuff with which we work are a more ultimate reality the apprehension of which constitutes our deepest knowledge of God. In the last resort, it would be more correct to say that the only God we make is the God we know. He will be a creature of distorted proportions if we have not learned to think his thoughts after him and to pattern conduct in conformity with divine standards as these are disclosed in the secrets of the real world in which our daily living is firmly imbedded.

For nineteen centuries Christianity has proclaimed that God is spirit. But too rarely has that spirit been allowed to dwell richly with mankind during the making of the daily historical process. God's activity has often been relegated to the beginning of some ideal procedure and made a miraculous and temporary insert into the world of common human experience. Ordinarily God does not travel the public highways of life but dwells apart in heavenly habitations. His interest in humanity is thought to be an affair of the past and future rather than of the present. He is supposed to have initiated long ago a program for man's salvation by an act of cosmic intervention, and he will complete the transaction by a final miracle of world renewal. But in the meantime he seems to have only a stepfatherly interest in the normal processes of history, and he is thought to be chiefly pleased with those persons who live freest from earthly entanglements.

The historian who works in the temper of modern scientific inquiry recognizes the conditions that produced this type of theistic imagery, and he appreciates the function it has served under the specific conditions of its origin and growth. But he is seeking a Deity who is integral to the normal historical process, knowledge of whom is derived from the observable phenomena of the world of human experience. His God is within, as well as above, his universe; and it is in his intimate relation to, and participation in, the processes of history that man comes closest to the Divine. Yet at the same time he reaches out toward the magnificent *tremendum* that lies beyond the ken of telescope and microscope and reveres the mysterious power generating and sustaining the physical world and its life. He pursues the ways of God as they are revealed by the inexorable laws of nature. In the human pursuit of moral and spiritual ideals that ever surge up within the spirit of mankind he recognizes the voice of the Deity speaking in divine accents to the souls of men. He holds that nothing that is now known or ever can be known in the realm of natural knowledge is impertinent or prejudicial to a true faith in God; and he lives in the confidence that, as knowledge grows from more to more, the reverence of mankind will ever enlarge.

C. THE LEISURE OF TIME

Man tends to become impatient with the tedium of time. Generation after generation grows old and dies, while the conflict between good and evil still rages unabated. The passing years seem oblivious to the struggle as they leisurely pile century upon century in the annals of history. If God has any concern with the historical process, why does he permit wickedness to continue indefinitely without suppression? This is a question often asked, either deliberately or subconsciously, by hosts of people when overtaken by evil days. They would make God an almighty superman whose patience with sinners had reached the breaking-point where he would ruthlessly smite them with the rod of his wrath. We humans often think we must believe in a God of vengeance, not only in order to maintain our conviction that the judge of all the earth must ultimately do right, but to compensate for our own weakness and frequent defeat in our struggles against the evils of the world.

When history is soberly viewed, it furnishes scant support for the existence of a vengeful Deity. In their zeal for justice prophets may forecast the early judgment of God upon sinful men or nations, and historians may cite instances illustrative of the divine displeasure. But a closer scrutiny of the historical process shows that disasters overtake equally the righteous with the wicked, and historical events said to constitute a display of divine justice never really have any permanent influence upon the suppression of sinners.

[211]

In our impatience to make God the champion of specific acts to restrain the evildoer, we fall into the unconscious habit of exhibiting the futility of allegedly divine interventions. So far as actual history attests the situation, it would appear that the Deity has not chosen to use violence to discipline mankind in the ways of righteousness. He does not resort to duress either to restrain sinners or to force men to do good works. He allows his sun to shine equally upon the evil and the good, and he pours down his refreshing showers upon both the just and the unjust. This was the conviction of the early Christians, who cited Jesus as authority for their opinion. So time flows on in its uninterrupted course, and the cause of righteousness remains unvindicated.

Sometimes we seek relief from the smothering burden of enduring time by painting a fanciful picture of the beginning and end of the historical process. We imagine that in the ideal days of human origins, when God was nearer to the earth, greater righteousness held sway. Also, in the not too far distant future he will, it is assumed, reassert his control and suppress evil. As far as the historian is concerned, these idealized pictures of both past and future are only visionary products of wishful thinking. As a matter of fact, the farther one's gaze penetrates into the dark recesses of time in the past, the more convinced does one become that good and bad have always been pitted against each other in the processes of human living. And he would be a visionary, indeed, who could imagine a time in the near future when the righteous will no longer be compelled to struggle desperately to resist evil.

Christians have been accustomed to treat too lightly the problem of eradicating evil from the human scene. Its origin is much more deeply seated in man's nature than our theologians have often imagined. This does not mean that Christians have been wont to wink tolerantly at sin but rather that they have failed to appreciate the intricate causes that have engendered and perpetuated human frailties. We used to be content to think that all evil was traceable to an Adamic taint stamped upon the race of mankind by its progenitor's infraction of a dietary rule imposed upon him by God. To eliminate evil we needed, so we supposed, only to nullify the effects of Adam's fall. But modern knowledge of the origins of the natural man has set the whole problem in a new framework and rendered its solution much more difficult. Now we know that the natural impulses of men stem from a brutish ancestry, and religion faces the herculean task of making moral and spiritual ideals flower above the beastly strain of savage blood inherited perhaps from a Neanderthal man. It is fortunate, indeed, that we have eons of time for the accomplishment of this gigantic task.

It is easy to become pessimistic when one chooses for companions the bad men of history. Their evil deeds have filled the life of humanity with dire distresses. Murderous hatreds have blighted the careers of men and nations. Greed has flourished; the quest for material possessions has mastered many lives; the strong have sorely oppressed the weak; while mercy and justice have been violently trampled under foot. The story of man's wickedness would fill volumes, even though only the first instalment could as yet be recorded. The bad men of tomorrow may add fiendish refinements to the techniques of their fathers, and the multiplicity of their doings shows no sign of diminishing. Their beastly blood still breeds true to type, while their animal emotions and appetites hold dominion over their souls.

As evil in its social expression is always the perverse act of some bad man, so every good that history finds realized in human society is the product of some good man's labor. Betterment depends not upon the miraculous insertion of some new quality or capacity into the existing universe but upon the operation of human intelligence, initiative, industry, and idealism in an effort to make more completely available the latent possibilities already resident in our world. The lightnings sported in the heavens from the dawn of time but remained useless for human good until a man arose to lay hold of them with Promethean cunning, to harness them to our machines, to make them light our dwellings, and to turn them into vocal messengers for carrying our thoughts around the globe. So it is in every area of cultural and spiritual attainment. God patiently waits for men to arise to the nobler heights of comprehension and accomplishment. From the narrow range of human vision this process may seem hopelessly slow, but from the point of view of God's enduring time there are still ages on ages available for future experiment and limitless growth.

History teaches us that God has chosen to work through the instrumentality of good men to effect the eradication of evil. Good people may seem to be a relatively small company, but they have rendered conspicuous service in bringing about the advancement of world culture from the dark days of primitive obscurity to the marvelous achievements of modern times. There is something about the activity of a good man that renders his work immortal even after the man himself has been quite forgotten. We may not know who first said: "Thou shalt not steal"; but there is a voice within us that attests the validity of the command. We recognize this to be for us an eternal truth, and the fact that we are able to apprehend it shows that we have been in communion with the God who sustains and permeates the historical process. Thus it happens that virtuous men of the past have left an undying heritage even when their lives were snuffed out by the overwhelming hostility of wicked contemporaries. No one could have suffered a more apparently overpowering calamity than that which overtook Jesus, and yet the clarity of his moral and spiritual insights glows ever more brightly with the passage of time. God works through the life of the good man who devotes himself to righteous causes.

When the Apostle Paul admonished the Philippians to work out their own salvation with fear and trembling under the conviction that God was accomplishing his will through their instrumentality, he was stating perhaps better than he knew the divine program for effecting the salvation of the world. Set in the framework of endless time, it gives us the key to the Christian philosophy of history. The future hope of the world rests with the activity of good men who recognize their responsibility as fellow-workers with God in shaping the processes of history. Slowly but surely they learn to read the story of his providential concern for human affairs in the life and work of mortals who struggle nobly to comprehend and control the rich resources of the universe. By striving to possess themselves of a man-mastered world they are brought into intimate contact with the Deity in whom they live and move and have their being. He is no absentee sovereign over the conflicts that are daily enacted on the human stage but is mankind's fellow-traveler upon both the highways and the byways that lead to the near and to the far-distant future.

There is mighty assurance in the fact that God is not pressed for time. One may entertain only a faltering faith in the competence of the mortal instruments through whom God acts within the observable processes of history. Even those men who most truly strive to know and do his will are often dull to perceive and slow to perform, and they are always destined for early death. Of them it must be said that their little systems have their day and are but broken lights of the larger wisdom that mankind craves. But the growth of righteousness, like all other manifestations of vital development in nature, is by increments so small that they can scarcely be seen with the naked eye; yet in the course of time the cumulative result may be almost colossal. In the struggle for righteousness limitless time stands conspicuously on the credit side of the ledger.

History to date is also reassuring. Even the casual observer realizes the tremendous spread of moral and spiritual interests over the earth during the last two thousand years. A gradually enlarging circle of mankind has learned to cherish ways of living that exemplify honesty, justice, and brotherly kindness. Men have caught new visions of what it means to cultivate both individual and social righteousness. They have been learning to make life conform to the new knowledge about God's universe that modern science has revealed, and in the light of this wisdom they have been able to take their place more intelligently and effectively as fellow-workers with God in the daily affairs of human living. In spite of the fact that evil men have multiplied their aggressions, the quest for the good life has increased its intensity as never before in the world's history. The struggle may grow more bitter, but goodness always thrives best under the strain of battle. Like the sapling that has matured under the whip of violent winds, so the fibers of righteousness grow strong to survive under the pressure of conflict. In this fact lies another ray of hope for the long future that still awaits human living.

What has been accomplished in the last twenty centuries is prophetic of vaster gains in the next twenty, or thirty, or one hundred centuries that lie ahead. The advances made in one generation may be scarcely perceptible, but the accumulations of the years mount ever upward toward the goal of the good man's desire as he seeks light and courage to pursue the divine way across the stage of earthly history. And the eternal God, working by slow degrees through frail human agents and continuing his activity over countless eons of time, insures the legitimate optimism of the Christian philosopher of history. The Kingdom of God cometh not with observation but by dint of strenuous endeavor on the part of men who serve him from generation to generation throughout the evolving centuries.

INDEX

Abraham, 16 f., 36, 108, 116, 189 f.

Activism, a human responsibility, 175 ff.

Alaric, 39, 152

Alexander the Great, 87, 135

Allen, E. L., 95

Antichrist, city of, 52

Aquinas, Thomas, 52 f., 197

Archeology, 58

Arianism, 166

Aristotle, 52, 148

Arnald of Villanova, 51

Athanasianism, 166

Aubrey, E. E., 98

Augustine, 32 f., 41 ff., 48, 108, 197

Augustus, Emperor, 46

Authority of the past, 3 f., 6, 157 ff.

Barnes, H. E., 78

Barth, Karl, 97 ff., 117, 179

Barth, Paul, 78

Bauer, W., 60

Beethoven, 3

Berdyaev, N., 102 ff.

Bernheim, E., 60

Bible, 149, 161, 169

Bishops, 36

Black Death, 152

Boniface VIII, 51

Bossuet, 54

Bristol, L. M., 78

Brunhes, J., 71

Buckle, H. T., 70

Bury, J. B., 78

Carlyle, Thomas, 64, 88

Charlemagne, 50

Christ, incarnation of, 47

Christianity, variations of, 166 f.

Church: Augustine's view of, 43; origin of, 172, 183; relation of, to the state, 37 f.; revelation in, 28 f.; rites of, 31; varieties of, 5 f.

Cicero, 135 f., 150, 152

City of God, 42 ff.

Civilization: amenities of, 138 ff.; collapse of, 133; origins of, 160; structure of, 131 ff.

Constantine, 34, 36; Donation of, 59

Crisis: cult of, 94 ff.; in religion, 176 ff.

Criticism: "higher," 62; "lower," 61

Crusades, 51, 128

David, 17 f.

Dawson, Christopher, 55

"Dialectical" method, 93 ff.

Diodorus, 150

Documents, study of, 57 ff.

Dodd, C. H., 116 ff.

Dogma, origin of, 172 f.

Donatists, 166

Eden, Garden of, 2

Ellwood, C. A., 78

Ethics, 173 f.

Eucharist, institution of, 116 f.

Euripides, 136

Eusebius, 34 ff.

Events, complexity of, 126 ff.

[219]